THE FIRST BOOK OF SELF-TESTS

Personal and Confidential Tests to Help You Learn More About Yourself

To Sharon:

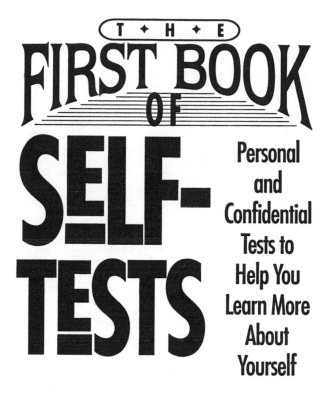

THE FIRST BOOK OF SELF-TESTS

Personal and Confidential Tests to Help You Learn More About Yourself

Rich Buhler and Dr. Gaylen Larson

A JANET THOMA BOOK

THOMAS NELSON PUBLISHERS
Nashville

About the Authors

Rich Buhler is the host of the nationally syndicated radio counseling program "Table Talk" which is broadcast live daily across the nation.

Dr. Gaylen Larson is founder/director of Alpha Counseling Center, Southern California's largest professional counseling service.

The anecdotes included in this book represent a composite of the stories of thousands of people and clients interviewed or counseled by Rich and Gaylen in their years of pastoral care and counseling. The names and circumstances of the individuals have been changed and any semblance of a character to someone in reality is purely coincidental.

The self-tests included in this book are in no way intended to be used as tools for diagnosis of conditions in a person's life and should not be used as a substitute for seeking a professional evaluation. Your answers merely suggest that, in some cases, you may want to consider seeking a professional evaluation or help.

TeleCounseling is a service that offers confidential professional counseling over the telephone no matter where you live. You can reach TeleCounseling by calling 800-225-0777.

Published in Nashville, Tennessee, by Thomas Nelson, Inc., and distributed in Canada by Lawson Falle, Ltd., Cambridge, Ontario.

Scripture quotations are from the NEW KING JAMES VERSION of the Bible. Copyright © 1979, 1980, 1982, Thomas Nelson, Inc., Publishers. Scripture quotations noted NASB are taken from THE NEW AMERICAN STANDARD BIBLE, Copyright © 1960, 1962, 1963, 1968, 1971, 1972, 1973, 1975, 1977 by The Lockman Foundation and are used by permission.

ISBN: 0-8407-3429-8

Printed in the United States of America
1 2 3 4 5 6—98 97 96 95 94 93

Contents

PART ONE: BEHAVIORS THAT CONQUER
Identifying Habits That Consume People's Lives

1. What's Going On Here?
   Testing Yourself or Someone Else about
   Conditions That Need to Be Identified and
   Solved   3

2. Is There an Alcoholic in the House?   11

3. Is Someone Popping Pills?
   The Grip of Legal and Illegal Drugs   19

4. Has Sex Become a Weapon?   31

5. When What You Eat Starts Eating You
   Food, A Common Addiction   39

6. Tall Tales and Exaggerations
   Habitual Lying   45

7. My Necklace Is Missing . . . Again
   Stealing   50

8. You're Too Close to Me
   Relationships That Stifle   57

9. The Odds Are Not in Your Favor
   An Addiction to Gambling   62

10. When the Going Gets Tough . . . The Tough Go
    Shopping
    The Shopaholics We Love   69

11. Planes, Trains, and Automobiles
    Hobbies and Recreational Activities That Run
    Amuck   74

12. The Biceps Tell It All
    When Exercise and Self-improvement Become a
    Bondage   78

13. The Accepted Addiction
    Workaholism   84

14. Putting God First
    Religious Addictions in the Lives of the Faithful   91

PART TWO: EMOTIONAL VOLCANOES
Feelings That Commonly Underlie
Addictions

---

15. Wasn't Grandpa Hot-Headed Too?
    When Anger Gets Out-of-Hand   101

16. It's All My Fault
    Guilt That Stands in the Way of Life   112

17. Afraid of the Dark
    When Fear Holds You Back   119

18. Everything Seems Gray
    When Depression Is a Companion   128

PART THREE: WHERE DID ALL THIS PAIN COME FROM?
The Importance of Recognizing Emotional Injury

19. I Always Thought It Was My Fault
    The Devastation of Sexual Abuse   137

20. My Folks Were a Little Strict, That's All,
    Identifying Physical Abuse   143

21. The Devil Did It to Me
    The Problem of Satanic Ritual Abuse   151

22. I Don't Remember Anything Before I Was Ten
    The Possibility of Repressed Trauma   159

PART FOUR: WHERE DO I GO FROM HERE?

23. What If I See Some of These Problems in My
    Own Life?   167

24. What If I See Some of These Problems in
    Another Person's Life?   172

Recommended Reading   179

Additional Resources   181

Support Groups   182

Additional Support and Recovery Groups   183

PART ONE:

Behaviors That Conquer

Identifying Habits That Consume People's Lives

What's Going On Here?

Testing Yourself or Someone Else about Conditions That Need to Be Identified and Solved

There's an old saying that warns, "You can't hit a bull's-eye unless you first know where to look for the target."

We believe, similarly, that you cannot find help for a problem from which you, a friend, or a loved one is suffering unless you first have a way of knowing what the problem is.

That's why we have put together this book of specific self-tests. If you've ever wondered whether you or someone you are concerned about may be suffering from an addiction or is the victim of a particular condition, you now have a way of examining that condition in a more precise way by considering some of the following pages.

Is this book a replacement for a complete psychological examination done by a professional clinician? No, in no way. However, it may prove very beneficial in helping you decide whether you or someone else should obtain such an evaluation.

Is this book a substitute for professional counseling by a licensed therapist? Again, no. However, by reading the true stories about people who have greatly benefited from recovery, you may become inspired to seek help.

This book is meant to be an avenue of discovery. It is focused on discoveries about you and other people who are hurting . . . who are hungering for understanding . . . who are buried in guilt . . . who are afraid . . . who are confused . . . who are emotionally alone . . . or who are spiritually frustrated.

As co-authors, we have combined experience of more than 40 years of work in the field of guidance and therapy. We have counseled literally thousands of people and have directed them toward recovery from a broad range of conditions.

Gaylen Larson is a licensed therapist, an ordained minister, and a doctor of psychology. He holds a B.A. in psychology and an M.A. in marriage and family relations from Azusa College, a B.S. in religious education from Life Bible College, and a Ph.D. in clinical psychology from Newport University. In 1974 he founded Alpha Counseling Center, which has expanded to thirty-four outpatient clinics in California and Arizona, a residential treatment center for teenagers, and two specialized inpatient programs for women. Dr. and Mrs. Larson have been married for twenty-three years and are the parents of two daughters. He is the author of *Too Much Is Never Enough* (San Diego, CA: Pacific, 1992).

Rich Buhler is a minister and author who is the host of "Table Talk," a daily talk-radio program carried nationwide via satellite. Since going on the air twelve years ago, Rich has had more than 70,000 one-on-one telephone conversations on the radio primarily with hurting people seeking his advice and has interviewed more than 7,000 guests. Rich holds B.A. and L.L.D. degrees from Biola University and is an ordained minister who has served in several pastoral positions, including seven years as senior pastor of a church in Long Beach, California. His previously published books are *Pain and Pretending; New Choices, New Boundaries;* and *Love . . . No Strings Attached.* He and his wife, Linda, are the parents of seven children.

As counselors we have met many people who are not resistant to discovering the truth about themselves. If there is a problem, these people want to know what it is and how to deal with it, but they have not been able to put a name to some of what they are experiencing.

For some readers, this book will provide ways of assessing the conditions and problems that exist in the lives of people around them (a spouse, child, parent, neighbor, friend, boss or co-worker). Other readers will use this book to help themselves become honest about their own lives. Either use is appropriate (and *both* can be done in total privacy).

Some of the most serious problems in our lives, or in the lives of people we care about, are problems we often are not fully aware of. Some of us may be completely blinded to an addiction or some other kind of condition that is causing pain to ourselves or to those who are close to us. Others of us may have a notion that there is some sort of problem, yet still minimize how serious it is or resist taking the steps that would solve it. This book will help you decide what, if any, steps you will need to take next in determining the severity of the problem.

This book is laid out in four sections. Each chapter in the first three parts contains a simple "test." The tests can be about you or about someone for whom you have a concern. These tests are not to be construed as any official diagnosis of any condition in your life or anyone else's life. They are merely tools to help you think seriously about the conditions that may be present.

You should not come to any formal conclusion as a result of these tests. If you suspect that you or someone you know is suffering from a problem that is described in one of the following chapters, it will be important for you to seek the help of professionals who know about those problems and who can meet with you and properly diagnose what's going on.

The first section of our book talks about some of the things that people do that they don't want to do, yet have a hard time trying to overcome. These things typically are addictions which people become enslaved to, which they cannot say no to, and which control the individual (drug abuse); obsessions, which tend to be thoughts that stay in the person's mind and are repeated over and over ("I'm a loser"); and compulsions, which are obsessive actions that people don't know why they do yet cannot stop doing (hand washing).

The second section of our book talks about some of the feelings that seem to be associated with addictions and emotional pain, related to fear, anger, depression, or similar problems.

The third section of the book explains some of the underlying conditions that may be responsible for causing the guilt, fear, anger or the addictive and destructive behaviors discussed in the earlier two sections. Those conditions are typically from emotional injury or emotional deprivation during early developmental years, such as physical, emotional, or sexual abuse or neglect or other kinds of loss or trauma. Incidents that have transpired during the very earliest years of life can be especially damaging.

An understanding of the underlying conditions helps us not only recognize the addiction or emotional problem, but also explores how such traumatic developments are fostered. In short, we go to the source, the root of the problem.

In today's culture, people typically tend to focus on the addictions and the behaviors that cause so much trouble and then they try to devote a lot of time and energy to overcoming them. However, as any alcoholic, drug addict, overeater or sexaholic can testify, it is very difficult to be successful on a long-term basis by just simply trying to "white knuckle it" in overcoming addictions. This is because the addictions are not the only problems. They are only symptoms of the problem; focusing just on symptoms will not lead to total recovery. The real objective is to discover what these things are symptoms *of*.

From our professional viewpoint, we believe they are often symptoms of deep emotional injury. And that is where the healing needs to take place and where much of the focus of getting help needs to occur.

The fourth section of the book will help direct you to the places you can get help if you have identified some of these symptoms in your own life or in the lives of others. We've included an appendix at the end of this section, which lists books and recovery and support groups where you can seek additional help for any problems you may discover as a result of reading this book.

INTO THE RECOVERY MODE

We'll talk a lot in this book about *recovery*, because where there has been injury there needs to be recovery. People tend to believe that anyone should be able to just "snap out of it" and either stop an addictive behavior or just "overcome" a paralyzing fear or crippling depression. Others hope for a "miracle" or look for some immediate solution that will bring success and healing and deliverance.

It's very important to recognize that at the very root of most of the conditions we will be talking about in this book there may be severe emotional injury. And, as previously stated, where there is injury, there needs to be recovery. But recovery almost always takes a season of time.

What, precisely, do we mean by *recovery?* Well, it can probably be best understood by comparing it to the aftermath of a physical injury. Most people respond to a person who has experienced physical injury by offering that person a great deal of compassion and understanding. If a person is seriously injured, there is an initial time of excruciating pain. This is followed by various stages of recovery, which can include crying, talking, dealing with anger, coping with restlessness, and being encouraged by friends and family members who sincerely care about the injured person's well-being.

It's very easy for us to accept the fact that an injury to bone, muscle, or flesh may require a sustained time of physical recovery; we know it will not last forever, and it doesn't have to be excruciatingly painful for the entire time. Nevertheless, it will probably take a season of time before the person can say, "I am well now. I have recovered."

The same thing is true of emotional injury. Whether it has been caused by molestation or emotional abuse or some other kind of trauma in childhood, or a more recent injury such as a rape, a career failure, or a divorce, people need a period of time to recover. That period of time will probably be longer than most of us expect. We need to be prepared for that.

We also need to offer understanding to others when recovery from emotional injury takes time for them.

Recovery is not simply surviving from day to day until enough time has passed so that we don't have to think about the problem anymore. Recovery is crying over what's never been cried about, getting angry about what's never been confronted before, praying about what's never been prayed about before, talking about what's never been talked about, and sometimes even feeling what may have not been felt for a long time or perhaps never felt at all.

That's what emotional recovery is all about. That's why having friends, support groups, and counselors are all important parts of recovery. Recovery should not be attempted alone.

You can imagine how harmful it would be, for example, if a woman who had lost her husband suddenly in a tragic accident decided to immediately close herself off emotionally and never to deal with that loss. She would be encasing herself in suspended shock. You can imagine some of the consequences that would result. If she remained that way for five or ten years and then suddenly realized she needed to overcome some of the problems her behavior had caused her, she would only then be entering the grieving period. Recovery would have been delayed all that time.

The point, once again, is that if there's been an emotional injury or a personal loss, there also needs to be a time of emotional recovery in order to deal with that injury or loss.

Children who have experienced childhood pain seldom had an opportunity to recover at the time the pain was inflicted. Children who have been physically, emotionally, or sexually abused, for example, have been typically abused by someone they knew and trusted, someone who would otherwise be the one to rescue them, to listen to them when they said something terrible happened, to believe them, to hold them, to let them cry, and to reassure them that they were not at fault.

If that support was never provided when the child was five

or six, it needs to be provided now, even though the person may be thirty or forty or fifty years old. That, in essence, is what recovery is all about.

WHERE YOU ARE NOW

Although some of the information presented in the following chapters could be applied to children, it has been assembled primarily with adults in mind. If you suspect that a child is suicidal or addicted to anything, or that he may have been abused in any way, it is important that you seek professional help for that child.

As an adult reader, you may discover in this book how events in your childhood caused problems that have surfaced since you've become an adult. It is important that you listen carefully to the lessons being presented in the chapters. Being older does not mean being wiser in regard to solving emotional problems. But we can help move you in the right direction.

Our goals are three-fold: (1) to help give you a name for the behavior or condition that may be causing a problem in your life or someone else's life; (2) to help you understand what it may mean about your life or another person's life; (3) to offer advice on how to get the proper kind of help for dealing with this condition.

Oddly enough, many things we will focus on in this book are considered good until they become problems. For example, eating is a good and necessary thing for human survival; however, food addictions can lead to a lot of problems, including, sometimes, death. Similarly, exercise is something good for physical health; however, when exercising becomes a nonstop addiction, it taxes the body beyond reasonable limitations.

We mention this as a caution, for we have seen situations wherein a person trying to overcome an addiction without entering into recovery will merely "swap" one problem for another. For example, a person addicted to smoking may feel "cured" because she hasn't had a cigarette in months, yet that same person may have suddenly become a food addict.

This is *not* a recovered person. Likewise, a person may have cut back on alcoholic consumption and feel as though the battle is over; but what he may not realize is that he has become a sexaholic or a prescription drug addict instead. This, too, is not a recovered person.

For adults, the reason an addiction is gripping is because it is almost literally the only thing they have left in their lives. There are many people for whom nothing seems to be working; nevertheless, in the midst of gorging themselves on food, they find a way of getting through another day; in the midst of addictive sex, they find a temporary way to blot out their problems; in the midst of spending money, they can experience some control; in the midst of investing themselves in a relationship or becoming a workaholic or drinking alcohol, they experience the only meaningful source of emotional nourishment they are capable of securing. The addiction or condition meets an emotional need in that person's life.

We hope to offer direction that will help break some of these negative addictions and harmful conditions you or someone you care about may be experiencing. We encourage you to use this book to take step one in solving whatever problem you are facing. Learn how to look for the bull's eye. Each of the following chapters will set up the target. Take your time, stay focused, and hit the mark.

Is There an Alcoholic in the House?

Jack London died at the age of forty. His kidneys failed. He had become the first author ever to earn one million dollars strictly from writing. He had been a sailor, gold prospector, newspaper reporter, rancher, politician and social reformer; he also had been a heavy drinker all his life.

Toward the end of his life, London wrote, "Circumstance was to continue to drive me toward John Barleycorn [whiskey], to drive me again and again, until, after long years, the time should come when I would look up John Barleycorn in every haunt of men—look him up and hail him gladly as benefactor and friend. And detest and hate him all the time. Yes, he is a strange friend, John Barleycorn" (*John Barleycorn*. New York: NAL/Dutton, 1990, chap. 6).

Such is the case with most alcoholics. They may recognize their addiction and hate it, yet they feel bound to stay tied to it until it ruins their lives or, as in Jack London's case, it kills them.

Alcoholism has caused a great deal of grief not only in the lives of alcoholics, but also in the lives of those who live or work with them. In today's mechanized society, alcoholics are also responsible for the deaths of thousands of innocent people each year because of drunk driving accidents. Alcoholics are a danger to themselves and to all of society. The problem is, sometimes neither society nor the alcoholics themselves are aware of what constitutes an addiction to alcohol.

Consider the story of "Jeff," who seemed to be the picture of success. He was popular and he was married to an equally popular woman named Cindy. Their kids were cute, their house was classy, and they were very comfortably set financially. Jeff had finished a graduate degree in his profession and he held a very respectable job. Jeff and Cindy were active in their church, where Jeff even held a position on the church board.

It was with a great deal of fear and reluctance that Cindy one day made an appointment with their pastor, Rev. Wilcott.

"I've really struggled with whether or not to come to talk to you about this," Cindy said nervously. "I love Jeff very much and I know that he has accomplished a lot of good things in his life and I am also aware of the fact that he is important to you and to the church. But I'm having a hard time knowing how to respond to some of his behavior."

"Tell me about it," Pastor Wilcott said encouragingly.

"Well, Jeff has a temper that he doesn't reveal in public," Cindy began. "For the first years of our marriage I only saw his temper flair up on occasional times, but lately it's been happening two or three times every week. It scares me and, even worse, it scares our children."

"Does any certain thing seem to set him off?"

"I've tried to figure that out," Cindy answered. "There really doesn't seem to be one particular thing that will set him off. Almost anything can trigger his temper anymore."

"Does it seem to occur at specific times or is it associated with anything else?" asked the pastor.

Cindy paused a moment, then nodded.

"Yes, it seems to happen most often in the evenings," she replied. "I guess he must be feeling a lot of stress at work or something, or maybe he's entering into a midlife crisis. When he gets home he usually needs a few drinks just to calm his nerves."

"How long has that been a part of his pattern? Does he rely on the drinks very often?"

"Jeff's always been the type of person to have some kind of drink in the evening," said Cindy. "At first it was just wine, but lately he's started having a few beers as well."

"Has it ever occurred to you, Cindy, that the way Jeff is acting may actually be a part of a problem that includes his use of alcohol?" asked Pastor Wilcott.

"Well, it crossed my mind once or twice," she admitted, "but then, Jeff is so dependable about work and church, I figured he couldn't be . . . well, you know. I mean, I've never seen him drink to the point of being too drunk to go to work or anything."

Pastor Wilcott, who was very familiar with the subject of alcoholism, asked Cindy a series of probing questions about Jeff that prompted him to conclude without any doubt that Jeff, indeed, was an alcoholic.

Being told this absolutely stunned Cindy. It was very difficult for her to associate the word *alcoholic* with the image she had of her handsome, successful husband. She had come to Rev. Wilcott to talk about what she viewed to be a problem with anger. Instead, Rev. Wilcott helped her understand that, although the anger was an important issue indicating there was a lot to deal with in Jeff's life, it was going to be important for her and Jeff to call the problem exactly what it was: *alcoholism.*

Rev. Wilcott used a ten-question quiz developed by Alcoholics Anonymous to help Cindy realize that even though Jeff was not getting horribly drunk during these episodes, he was experiencing mood changes because of his drinking. Cindy had been so depressed over Jeff's behavior and so concerned about what was going on, it had been difficult for her to realize the true purpose of his drinking. He was *not* taking a drink only to calm his nerves. He was dulling his feelings and getting away from whatever for him had been painful about work or about home or about life in general. And the result was that the enormous anger inside of him that he normally kept under control was suddenly set loose.

Many of the people in our culture are not aware of the fact that alcoholics come from all backgrounds and ethnic groups, and from both sexes. It used to be that a person thought of an alcoholic as being a middle-aged man with a stubby beard, living on skid row and carrying his booze around with him in a bottle concealed in a brown paper bag. Each of us has a picture in our mind of what we think an alcoholic is. When someone does not fit that picture, it is hard for us to think of that person as being an alcoholic, even if all the classic signs of alcoholism may be there.

It is well known that alcoholics tend to be in denial about how serious their problem may be. It is just as true, however, that members of the family or co-workers or friends of an alcoholic downplay the seriousness of what is going on in that person's life.

Here is a list of statements that you can ask about yourself or about another person who is important to you that may suggest whether some help should be sought regarding a possible drinking problem. Put a check mark before each statement that is true.

Is There a Problem with Alcohol?

☐ 1. This person has decided to stop drinking for a period of time but has not had permanent success.

☐ 2. There are people in this person's home who feel this person's drinking is a problem.

☐ 3. There are people at this person's job who consider this person's drinking to be a problem.

☐ 4. This person has missed days of work or school because of drinking.

☐ 5. This person's drinking is interfering with relationships with a spouse or children.

☐ 6. This person has committed or has considered committing an immoral or illegal act because of drinking.

☐ 7. This person has had to borrow money or sell items because of drinking.

☐ 8. This person's drinking occurs on occasions of being angry or upset as a way of dealing with worry or trouble.

☐ 9. Drinking is controlling portions of this person's life.

☐ 10. This person wrestles with guilt or remorse because of drinking.

☐ 11. This person has been arrested, threatened with arrest, or has gotten into legal trouble because of drinking.

☐ 12. This person compromises the quality of friendships or associations because of drinking.
☐ 13. This person has lied or covered up because of drinking.
☐ 14. This person sometimes sincerely promises others that he or she will stop drinking, but without success.
☐ 15. This person drinks in secret.
☐ 16. This person resists suggestions that his or her drinking is a problem and wishes that people would mind their own business.
☐ 17. This person has experimented with switching from one kind of drink to another in order to avoid drunkenness.
☐ 18. This person has to have a drink as an "eye opener" on some mornings.
☐ 19. This person tries to get extra drinks at a party because of a feeling of not getting enough.
☐ 20. This person has had blackouts caused by drinking.

If you recognized yourself or someone else in the previous list of statements and if you marked three or more, it is probably a good idea to get a professional evaluation as to whether or not alcohol has become a problem in your life or someone else's.

RECOGNIZING THE ADDICTION

One of the most important things to remember about any person with an addiction is that the person will almost always either deny that the problem exists or will diminish the importance of it in his or her mind. This denial occurs despite the evidence of the addiction and the danger of it.

In the case of alcoholism, it is also important to remember that when a person is drunk, he or she is emotionally living in a different world and will either not remember some of what has occurred while drunk or will not remember it the same way as those who are sober.

It is very frustrating to confront an alcoholic about the seriousness of his or her behavior because that person will not only have a natural tendency to deny the existence or the severity of the problem, but may actually not have an accurate memory of some of the things that occurred while drunk. In Jeff's case, for example, he imagined that his taking a few drinks was making things better, and he did not recognize that he was dishing out abuse to his wife and children.

One major misunderstanding about alcoholism is the belief that alcoholics either always get drunk when drinking or get drunk on a daily or weekly basis. Anyone who is getting drunk routinely, of course, has a problem and should seek help for it. It is not uncommon, however, for a person to have an addiction to alcohol that may manifest itself only every few weeks or months or so. The key is whether the incident happened more than once or twice and whether the person seems to be dependent on alcohol and whether he or she feels guilt and tries to conceal what has happened.

Gordon Brodersen, a certified Marriage, Family, Child Counselor (MFCC) with Alpha Counseling, has spent many years working with alcoholics entering recovery. The child of an alcoholic father, Brodersen has experienced alcoholism firsthand. Gordon graduated from Pacific Christian College and worked as a youth pastor and then for twenty years as an elementary school teacher. In 1974 he completed a master's degree in psychology at Pepperdine University and has been a professional counselor since then.

"There are a lot of reasons why people turn to alcohol," says Gordon. "Sometimes it's environment. If you've grown up in a family in which everyone drinks alcohol and you are not condemned if you do, too, then you probably will. Other times, as with the case of many teenagers, it's a matter of peer pressure. You don't want to be the only one who doesn't drink at a party. You want to fit in."

Gordon notes that a lot of teenagers will experiment with alcohol yet never become alcoholics. Research shows that up to 90 percent of high school seniors have taken their first drink. While many will not develop a drinking problem, approximately 3.3 million American teens, ages fourteen to seventeen, were showing signs of serious drinking problems during the early 1990s. At the opposite end of the spectrum, nearly 15 percent of all Americans over the age of sixty were becoming or were already alcoholic (many times motivated by the loss of a spouse or failing health).

"When I counsel young people who have developed a drinking problem, I note a lot of common problems in all of their lives," explains Gordon. "These kids have started to live by three silent rules: don't talk, don't feel, don't trust. This is because they have come from very dysfunctional families."

Among the common problems faced by teenage alcoholics are these seven points shared by Gordon Brodersen:

(1) No opportunities exist for the child to express feelings.
(2) The child is embarrassed by his or her parents.
(3) The parents break promises and tell lies to the child.
(4) The parents' anger is unpredictable.
(5) There is physical and verbal abuse (or sexual abuse).
(6) Punishment for behavior is inconsistent.
(7) Punishments are far more severe than warranted.

Many times the only reason an alcoholic will seek help is because he or she was forced to do so. A drunk driver may get in trouble with the law or a spouse may threaten to leave or a school may warn of expulsion unless this person seeks counseling.

"When people come for counseling, we never promise to cure them," says Gordon Brodersen. "We approach alcoholism as a disease that needs to be controlled. You control it, you don't shake it. Even someone who has been sober twenty years can relapse. Our job is to provide the individual with some coping skills during the first year. Slowly, in time, we will seek the source of the deeper problem that has led to the alcoholism. Recovery is a steady, not an overnight process. And we don't always succeed. Fortunately, however, we *often* succeed."

SUMMARY

We noted several specific things in this chapter. We discovered that alcoholism is not limited to the stereotyped drunk in the alley image, but is instead something that can affect people in all walks of life from all varieties of backgrounds. We noted that alcoholics are not only a detriment to themselves and their families, but also to people they work with and to people they may injure through incidences of drunk driving. Whether they enter into recovery voluntarily or are forced into it, counseling and support groups are the best route for an alcoholic.

Is Someone Popping Pills?

The Grip of Legal and Illegal Drugs

It's amazing that even though drug abuse has been given a lot of visibility, it is still very widespread. Part of the problem, of course, is that there are those who will use drugs and who will become addicted to drugs no matter how many warnings are issued.

Another part of the problem, however, is that there are a lot of people addicted to drugs who don't realize it. One of the skills of an addict is denial—either denying the addiction exists or minimizing how bad it is. There are also a lot of friends and family members of addicts who, even though they know a legal or illegal drug is being used, may not have come to the recognition of it as a problem.

The popularity of various illegal drugs comes and goes. At the time of this writing, the old psychedelic drugs of the 1960s are making a comeback. Cocaine is a serious problem. Regardless of the substances that are being used, however, the impact of people's lives is similar and devastating, and the challenge of admitting that there is a dependency on drugs is an intense one to accept, both for the addict and the people in the addict's life.

Of additional importance are the widespread addictions to prescription drugs. Multitudes of people are hooked on legal medications either innocently or knowingly, and it is especially difficult for someone in that category to recognize the problem because they feel that if it's legal it's probably not a problem.

Look at what you see—row after row of eye drops, nasal sprays, cough drops and cough syrups, antihistamine tablets, aspirin and aspirin substitutes, iodine, mercurochrome, rubbing alcohol, decongestant pills, mouthwash, ear wax dissolvent, epsom salts, throat gargle, blister salves, liniment rubs, toothache poultices, sunburn ointments, stomach acid tablets, dandruff shampoos . . . the array of medications seems endless.

Access to drugs is not a problem in this country. Not only are these drugs legal and mass produced and competitively priced, they also are *promoted*. Patent medications are advertised on radio and television, in newspapers and magazines, on billboards, and through mail-order coupons and trial-size bottles.

Americans grow up being encouraged to pop a pill to solve this problem and to swallow a tablet to cure that problem. As people build up a tolerance to common painkillers, the companies market more potent pills: 200 mg., 350 mg., 500 mg. The cure-all anthem seems to be that "bigger is better" and "if one is good for you, four must be even better."

In light of all this, it's no surprise to learn that many people—good people who would *never* think of buying marijuana or cocaine from a drug pusher—wind up addicted to prescription medications. It's not that great a jump from being a consumer of vast amounts of over-the-counter drugs to becoming a consumer of doctor-prescribed drugs.

If you have begun to worry that maybe you have become dependent on certain drugs, or if you suspect that someone you care about may have a drug addiction, take a moment now to respond to the following test. Put a check mark before each statement that is true.

Is There a Problem with Drugs?

❏ 1. This person has decided to stop using medications for a period of time but has not been successful.

❏ 2. There are people in this person's home who feel this person has a problem with drugs.

❏ 3. There are people at this person's place of employment who feel this person has a drug problem.

❏ 4. Friends have told this person they think he or she has a problem with drug dependency.

❏ 5. This person has missed days at work or school because of drugs.

❏ 6. This person has committed (or considered committing) an illegal or immoral act because of drugs.

❏ 7. This person has sold personal possessions or borrowed money in order to purchase drugs.

❏ 8. This person's use of drugs is a way of dealing with worry, anger, or loneliness.

❏ 9. This person uses drugs as a way of escaping pressure from the job or a bad home life.

❏ 10. This person feels guilt and remorse about drug use.

❏ 11. A dependency on drugs has started to control a part of this person's life.

❏ 12. This person has been arrested or threatened with arrest because of an involvement with drugs.

❏ 13. Since starting to use drugs, this person's personality has changed.

❏ 14. This person has lied to cover up drug use.

❏ 15. This person uses drugs secretly and keeps a hidden supply of extra drugs stashed away.

❏ 16. This person has promised to stop using drugs but has not yet done so.

❏ 17. This person has switched from one drug to another in the hope that this would shake a dependency.

❏ 18. This person has gone to more than one doctor in order to get a prescription for the same drug.

❏ 19. This person has forged a prescription in order to get drugs.

❏ 20. This person has taken drugs from someone else's medicine cabinet or has asked another person to refill a prescription and turn it over to him or her.

Now, let's take a moment to consider your responses. We do not want you to consider this twenty-question quiz to be a substitute for a complete physical examination by a physician or a psychological analysis by a licensed therapist; however, looking at your responses may help you decide whether you or someone you care about needs to take this next step.

If you marked any of those statements, we urge you to put some serious thought into what it means about this person's life. Obviously, the more statements you marked, the more it means there may be a problem and the need for some kind of professional evaluation to know for sure.

Consider the story of Josh. Josh was a partner in a successful automobile dealership, and from all appearances was pursuing the American dream of success. He and his wife and two daughters lived in a comfortable neighborhood, had a good reputation, and were active in their church. Josh was known as the kind of person you could count on for help when you needed it.

Josh's wife Karin considered herself fortunate to have a husband who was a good provider and respected by his friends, so she became alarmed when, after fifteen years of marriage, he seemed to be changing. The differences were subtle at first. Josh started doing some uncharacteristic things, like changing his wardrobe and becoming involved in some sporting activities that had never appealed to him before. At first Karin thought, "Who cares? Josh's just approaching midlife and is developing some new interests."

What concerned Karin, however, was the fact that along with these new activities Josh seemed to have less interest in his family and was somewhat aloof emotionally. When Karin tried to address her fears, Josh became irritated and accused her of imagining too much.

Then Josh started making exotic purchases he and Karin could not afford. He bought an expensive sailing boat, for example, and along with it an exclusive sports car. Karin protested loudly, but to no avail. Josh wouldn't consider her warnings that their budget just couldn't handle his new, expensive tastes.

Most alarmingly, Karin discovered that Josh was cultivating a friendship with a woman who was a member of the sailing club he had joined. She also expressed her concerns about that to Josh, but he convincingly declared that there was no danger that he would ever be more than a fellow club member with the woman, and he made it clear that he resented Karin's thinking otherwise.

Josh's life began to deteriorate rapidly. His business partners became exasperated with him because, they said, he had ceased to live in the real world and insisted on making some of the same perplexing financial decisions at work that he was making at home. The partners began to take steps to remove themselves from the business. At the same time, Josh was discovered spending the weekend on his boat with the woman from the sailing club. Karin promptly asked him to move out of the house. To make matters worse, when Karin suspiciously started looking into Josh's telephone calls, credit card purchases, and other spending records, she found that he had been having a relationship with this other woman for a long while and had spent thousands of dollars of his savings and had taken out a mortgage on their home that she knew nothing about.

Karin went to her pastor in desperation and spilled the entire story, a tale she had been reluctant to tell because she didn't want people at the church to think that she and Josh were anything other than the happy couple that people thought they were.

The pastor happened to be a person who had special training and knowledge in substance abuse and had previously been a drug counselor. From what Karin told him, he strongly suspected Josh was using drugs.

The pastor met with Karin, her children, the partners in the business, and Josh's older brother and suggested they do an intervention: a professional procedure that effectively confronts the addict with the seriousness of the problem and insists that he agree to get help.

One evening when Josh dropped by the house at Karin's request, he found the pastor and all the other friends and family sitting in his front room waiting for him, and they conducted a firm but loving intervention in his life. They told him he was on the verge of losing everything that was important to him if he didn't take some steps to deal with whatever was going on.

Josh was thunderstruck. He reluctantly agreed to enter a professional hospital program to seek counseling, and it was there that it was revealed that he had been using cocaine for quite some time.

Like many cocaine addicts, Josh had begun his relationship with cocaine because a friend of his said it would help him do a better job at the business. Josh, who had always heard horror stories about cocaine, was surprised at how good he felt when he used it. He convinced himself that it was not having the bad effect on him that he thought it had on other people. The more he used it, the more he became dependent on it and the more he lived in a world that was formed and sustained by the use of the drug. It nearly destroyed his home, his business, and his life.

THE SUBTLE SICKNESS—THE PROBLEM WITH PRESCRIPTION DRUGS

Drug dependency sometimes develops over so long a period of time, the victim may not be aware of it until it is too late.

Consider the situation, for example, of Abby. After going through a long and difficult divorce that left her penniless, jobless, and homeless, Abby found herself a single parent and out on the street. With money borrowed from relatives, she set up a small typesetting business. For two years she worked 15-hour days building up a clientele and paying off debts.

Right after her divorce, Abby had been given a prescription by her family doctor for tranquilizers. They helped Abby through periods of anxiety when she would worry about how she and her daughter were going to eat, pay for an apartment, and buy a car. Abby used over-the-counter sleeping aids to help her rest at night too. If the sleeping pills didn't act quickly enough, she'd take a tranquilizer with them.

When she began her business, Abby's worries increased: Would her creditors be patient? Would her customers come back again? Should she spend her first profits on more advertising? Could she save money by not buying insurance, or would that be too risky?

It helped to take a few tranquilizers during the day in order to calm her nerves. So as not to draw attention to how often she was getting her prescription refilled, Abby went to two different doctors for prescriptions. On one occasion she altered the prescription so that the number of pills provided was doubled.

Another time, Abby discovered that a cousin of hers had once taken the same tranquilizers, so Abby asked the cousin to refill her order but to give the pills to Abby. The cousin did it because she could get the pills free under her insurance plan. She didn't know that Abby was already being supplied by another druggist.

Abby went so far as to visit a different doctor where she was given another prescription for a different kind of tranquilizer. She began to take both types. She would horde huge supplies of them so that if anyone ever caught onto her schemes, she would still have an adequate stash of pills to get her through any crisis.

It didn't really occur to Abby that she had become a drug addict. She rationalized that any pill prescribed by a doctor had to be safe. After all, doctors would never harm you. In fact, if anything, doctors underprescribed medicines just to be on the safe side. (This is why she felt justified in increasing her dosages. She knew what she could "handle.")

To counteract the stupor she felt each morning from the sleeping pills and tranquilizers, Abby began to take over-the-counter pills containing huge doses of caffeine. She also drank many cups of coffee and several soft drinks (not caffeine-free) during the day.

Abby's personality began to alter. She became very demanding of her daughter. She starting acting impatient with her customers. She became belligerent with her suppliers of paper and inks. She was rude to her friends and neighbors.

For a time, people made excuses for Abby's behavior. She was just overworked . . . she was feeling the stress of being a single parent . . . she was going through early menopause . . .

she hadn't had a date in a long time . . . she was not taking time to eat balanced meals.

Abby's teenaged daughter begged her mother to visit their pastor or their doctor for help. Abby told her that children should not meddle in the affairs of adults.

Eventually, Abby's dependency on prescription drugs created such continuous physical and emotional problems for her, she could not keep up with her work at the print shop. Without telling anyone, she made an appointment with a counselor who, in turn, directed her to a drug rehabilitation program. She received medical attention and emotional counseling.

With love, support, and encouragement from her daughter and friends, Abby broke her addiction. It took time and it wasn't easy, but she did it.

For others, however, the ending isn't always as rosy. Some addictions lead to lost time at work, nervous breakdowns, physical ailments, even death.

We know of one incident wherein an eighth grade girl brought two of her friends home after school. The girl's mother was on a prescription drug for a sustained ailment she was battling. She worked part-time in the afternoons. The girls had heard stories about the "rush" that drugs called "uppers" could give kids. They decided to take one pill each out of the mother's prescription bottle.

To their surprise, the pills didn't cause them to be hyped-up or to see psychedelic visions. However, the pills did kill all pain. The girls felt lazy and warm and peaceful. They didn't worry about homework assignments or their divorcing parents or their acne problems or school popularity contests or *anything*. They just sat in a room, listening to the radio and snuggling next to stuffed animals. It was wonderful.

That weekend the girls met again and shared the same experience. Again, it seemed blissful. The personal, family, and school problems the girls were facing seemed inconsequential while they were under the influence of the drug. Soon, they experimented with drugs from the medicine cabinets of the other two girls' parents. By high school they were buying illegal drugs and were full-blown addicts. What started as a flirtation with prescription drugs led to a tragic dependency on narcotics.

UNEXPECTED SIDE EFFECTS

When we think of these three girls or even of Abby, we realize that although there is a degree of innocence here, in that most people feel that prescription drugs cannot harm them, there also is a measure of guilt; after all, these people were either taking drugs that had not been prescribed to them or they were not following the physician's recommended dosage. There is another victim of prescription drug abuse, however, who is totally innocent. This is the person who becomes addicted to prescription drugs even though he or she *is* following the doctor's orders.

This latter problem has existed for centuries. During the Civil War, for example, the drug morphine seemed to work miracles for it could stop all feeling, even in amputees. As such, if a wounded soldier experienced pain, he was given morphine. The soldier recovered from his wounds but then discovered he was addicted to morphine. Many centuries before that, the Chinese had the same experience with opium.

Rich Buhler knew a pastor whose entire life was ruined because of an addiction to prescription drugs. Sadly, neither the pastor nor his doctor recognized the side effects caused by the drug until they manifested themselves as a complete breakdown of the man's physical and psychological order.

This pastor had never had a problem with substance abuse. He didn't overeat or smoke or drink alcohol or use drugs. His only addiction was work, and even that was motivated by his genuine love for his congregation. He loved to preach, teach, visit his families in their homes, work with the church boards, and counsel folks who were having problems. His congregation grew very large, and it became obvious that the pastor really needed an associate to help carry the work load. But, no, he just decided to work that much harder.

As might be expected, the poor, overworked pastor finally

reached a point of burnout. His board of elders lovingly "ordered" him to take a few days off and to get a complete physical. The pastor saw the wisdom in this.

The doctor said there was nothing seriously wrong with him, but he did feel that the pastor should cut back on his work load. He gave him some sedatives to help him relax, some sleeping pills in case he couldn't rest at night, and some vitamin supplements to rebuild his stamina.

Having never used much medicine in his life, the pastor didn't recognize that the pills he started taking were having an abnormally strong effect on him. Within a short period of time the pastor could not sleep unless he took one or two of the sleeping pills. He also found that unless he used one of the sedatives at midmorning and after lunch, he would get headaches. However, since by using the pills he was able to sleep and work, he felt they were working. In reality, he was becoming more and more addicted to the pills.

The pastor had occasional follow-up appointments with his doctor, but for some reason the effect of the medication was never fully recognized. Within a few months, the pastor was having problems with his memory and his attention span. He also had trouble organizing his thoughts. His sermons were vapid, his talks were unfocused, his board meetings were loose. The people in the congregation wondered if the man had a drinking problem or was suffering from Alzheimer's Disease.

As the pastor's condition worsened, the elders had no choice but to notify him that he was being relieved of his authority: he was fired. Two days later he collapsed in his home and was rushed by ambulance to the hospital. He was diagnosed there as being addicted to prescription drugs.

The pastor was ashamed and emotionally devastated by this news, even though he was perfectly innocent of the cause of the problem. The pastor's congregation was equally innocent. Since the pastor had not informed anyone that he was taking medication that might cause noticeable side effects, his people had been at a loss in trying to come up with a reason for the pastor's odd behavior. The people in the congregation had responded in quite a predictable way: they didn't know what was wrong, but they did know the pastor was dysfunctional. He could no longer manage church business nor minister to the people. He had to be replaced.

This scenario is typical of prescription drug addictions. They are always progressive, and usually a sign of an addiction is when a life is out of balance in one or more major areas. There's always a price to pay—a lost career, a damaged relationship, perhaps even a physical injury.

That's one of the tests as to whether or not a person is addictive: what kind of harvest is occurring in that life as a result of that problem? If a person ignores important priorities of personal health, of family, of friends, of employment, and of faith just so that he or she can participate in a recurring behavior, this activity is probably an addiction.

FACING THE PROBLEM

If you or someone you are trying to help is dealing with a potential or existent problem with prescription drug addiction, let us offer some helpful suggestions:

- Never vary from the specific instructions issued by the doctor regarding the use of medication.
- If you are consulting the advice of more than one physician, make sure each one is aware of the treatment of the other.
- Never use medications prescribed for another person.
- Notify your supervisor at work of anyone you are sure is abusing drugs.
- Never mix medications at random.
- If you have been using over-the-counter medications, ask your doctor about whether to continue or discontinue the usage.
- If you cannot shake your dependence on prescription drugs, seek help from your physician or a local drug treatment center or a licensed therapist.
- Support drug awareness and drug education programs in your schools, neighborhoods, youth clubs, churches, and hospitals.

In an effort to make yourself more aware of the ways drugs and chemicals have an effect on the human body, we recommend that you consult the books listed in Recommended Reading on page 179.

4

Has Sex Become a Weapon?

In the 1991 motion picture *City Slickers*, one of the male characters says to his friend, "Women need a reason for sex. Men need a place."

This was apparently close enough to the truth, though obviously exaggerated, because it caused a lot of laughs in the movie theater. The stereotypical male is usually portrayed as always eager for sex, and the stereotypical female is usually portrayed as trying to avoid sex. Both are extreme, incorrect descriptions for most people. However, there are some people of both sexes who are absolutely addicted to sex.

Like many other addictions, sexual addictions are a problem of a normal appetite gone wrong. The hunger for sex is God-given but like the hunger for food, which is also God-given, it can become a drive that is rooted in more than just the biological need to have closeness or sexual release or to reproduce.

For the sexual addict, sex is more than just one of the many sources of pleasure in life. Instead, it is bigger than life. Sex is, in some respects, life itself.

Sexual addictions can vary. Some sexual addicts have repeated sexual relationships. Others are addicted to pornography or sexual conversation. Still others, such as "Peeping Toms," are addicted to invading other people's private lives. Some find it difficult to think about anything other than sex.

If you've wondered whether you or someone you care about may have a sexual addiction, read the following list of statements. Put a check mark before each statement that is true.

Is There a Problem with a Sexual Addiction?

☐ 1. Sexual activity controls portions of this person's life.
☐ 2. This person thinks of sex most of the time.
☐ 3. This person has decided to stop unwanted sexual activity for a period of time but without permanent success.
☐ 4. There are people in this person's home who consider this person's sexual activity to be a problem.
☐ 5. There are people at this person's place of employment who consider this person's sexual activity to be a problem.
☐ 6. This person is known to make others feel uncomfortable or violated because of unwanted sexually oriented conversation.
☐ 7. This person has lost time at work or school because of sexual activity.
☐ 8. This person has committed or considered committing an illegal or immoral act because of a sexual addiction.
☐ 9. This person feels guilt or remorse because of sexual activity.
☐ 10. This person takes refuge in sexual activity to escape the troubles and people around him or her.
☐ 11. This person has been arrested or been threatened with arrest or gotten into legal trouble because of sexual activity.
☐ 12. This person compromises the quality of friendships or relationships because of sexual activity.
☐ 13. This person has lied or covered up because of sexual activity.
☐ 14. This person sometimes sincerely promises others that he or she will stop the sexual activity but without permanent success.
☐ 15. This person does sexual activities in secret.
☐ 16. It seems that sex and sexual temptation or stimuli are controlling this person's life.
☐ 17. This person's sexual activity occurs on occasions of being angry or upset or as a way of trying to deal with worry or trouble.
☐ 18. This person keeps going from one relationship to another.
☐ 19. This person feels like getting away from a sex partner as soon as possible after having sex.
☐ 20. This person seems to be addicted to other sexual activities, such as viewing pornography or trying to observe other people in intimate settings by being a "Peeping Tom."

If you marked two or three of these statements, we urge you to put some serious thought into what it means about this person's life. Obviously, the more statements you responded yes to, the more there is a possibility of a problem and the need for some kind of professional evaluation. If you marked five or more statements, you should probably seek a professional evaluation.

IS IT AN ADDICTION?

Sexual addicts cannot simply be considered people who have "no willpower" or "no morals," as many in our culture believe. There are many sexual addicts who do value moral conduct. In fact, some addicts, habitually engaging in sexual activity in their secret lives, are known, publically, to have rigid sexual standards.

Similarly, sexual addiction cannot be simply defined as "any activity that is considered immoral or illegal." Immoral or illegal activity is frequently associated with sexual addiction, but sexual addiction can also be acted out under typically acceptable conditions. Sexual intercourse within marriage, for example, is universally accepted. But there are some sexual addicts who overpower and torment and victimize their own spouses. The key to knowing if a person is sexually addicted is, as with other addictions, knowing if the sexual activity seems to be driven, if it is accompanied by guilt, if it is at the expense of the feelings and needs of others, if it is causing trouble in the life of the addict, and if it is out of control.

Michael is an example of a person who appeared to be happy, moral, and healthy, but who was consumed with sexual themes and activities that were addictions and the result of his own victimization.

NO ONE EVER SUSPECTED

Michael was a professional artist. He and his wife, Lorraine, had their ups and downs, but both were likable people and had a lot of friends. They loved children and were well known for their work in their church and in their neighborhood.

What a lot of people at church did not know was that Michael was a multiple addict. For years he had been an alcoholic, the kind who virtually never got drunk but who consumed enough alcohol every evening to escape the pain of life. Recently, Michael had cut back on his drinking, but then had become hooked on marijuana. Only Lorraine and a few close friends knew of Michael's addiction to pot. But even Lorraine did not know Michael was also a sexual addict.

As a teenager, Michael became addicted to masturbation. He impulsively masturbated several times a day and almost anywhere he could find to do it: in restrooms, in closets at school, in his car when he was driving alone. All his sexual experiences were alone, but in his secret world he was obsessed with it. He described himself as not being able to go for more than a few minutes without having some sexual thought or retreating into a sexual fantasy or thinking about people around him in sexual terms.

When Michael went to college and was away from home for the first time, he discovered hard-core pornography and sexually oriented bookstores and theaters. He didn't want to ruin his reputation as a clean-cut guy, so he traveled to a city more than one hundred miles from his college so he could indulge in the pornography.

The most troubling part of Michael's addiction was his urge to molest, to sexually violate, children, especially boys.

Michael had grown up in a large family and had stepped across the line of molestation several times with younger siblings and also when he had babysat as a teenager. As an adult, he had not often molested a child. When he did, he was consumed with guilt and swore to himself and to God it would never happen again. Michael lived in terror that someone would eventually discover what he had done or that one of the children he had molested would reveal his conduct.

It was Lorraine's frustration with Michael's addiction to marijuana that led to his seeking help. Michael's wife finally got fed up because Michael was almost always using pot.

When he wasn't using, he seemed to be living in another world.

Lorraine got tired of having a sexual relationship each evening with a person floating around in the clouds because of drugs. She also got weary because it was in that condition that he usually wanted to have sex and she felt used. Lorraine insisted that Michael get counseling. And after a long period of time, he agreed to go.

"I was embarrassed to seek counseling," Michael said. "But a part of me knew that I needed it—there were so many loose ends in my life. I established a good relationship with my counselor. I talked about my childhood and some of the emotional complexities of my life and my addiction to pot. But I never talked about the sex. Nobody knew about it, so why bring it up? I was hoping that, because I was in counseling, I could conquer it by myself." Disaster struck when one of the boys from Michael's family revealed he had been molested by Michael.

Michael's brother had so many emotional problems his family had sought professional help for him. The boy's counselor saw evidences that the boy had been molested and had pursued the evidence until the truth was revealed.

County authorities appeared at Michael's door one day after that and told Michael he was being investigated for child molestation.

"I was shattered," Michael reflected. "My worst nightmare had come true and I was sure that my life and my marriage were finished. My wife was shocked and angry, and my friends were in disbelief.

"It turned out to be the best thing that ever happened to me, though. The investigation forced me to be real with myself about my problems and to be more honest with my counselor."

Michael, not surprisingly, was a victim of molestation himself, though he had never told anyone. An older brother had molested him over a period of several years, beginning when Michael was six.

"I had filed all of that away in the recesses of my mind,"

Michael said. "I felt so guilty—like it was my fault—that I just tried to get through each day of my childhood as best I could without thinking about it. There was probably not a day, though, that I didn't wonder about sex and what my being victimized meant about me."

Michael courageously committed himself to recovery and to dealing with the roots of his addictions. He and Lorraine became closer as a result. And Michael has since become a popular speaker on the subject of sexual victimization and a leader of church ministry of support groups for sexual addicts and victims of sexual molestation.

Other sexual addicts, unlike Michael, do not keep their addiction hidden. Instead, their addiction is part of their identity.

ALWAYS THE PLAYBOY

Rich Buhler once worked at a radio station with a man we'll call Warren, who was a sexual addict. Warren would never have identified his behavior as an addiction. He was, in fact, proud of his conquests.

Warren considered himself God's gift to women and made it a point to tell them that. He openly invited the women who worked at the station to have sex with him, and he bragged about those who accepted. The women who would not have sex with Warren, he harrassed with sexual remarks.

Warren rarely had more than a two- or three-minute conversation with anyone without making sex the subject or seasoning the discussion with sexual innuendos. Many of the women at the station were, of course, infuriated by Warren's conduct and confronted him. But Warren simply responded by making them his more frequent targets. It never seemed to end.

This all happened about twenty years ago. Such behavior today would warrant charges of sexual harrassment and serious consequences.

As far as Rich knows, Warren never realized his life was defined by sex or admitted his addiction. The last Rich heard, Warren was still not married and was still unable to have anything that resembled an intimate and healthy relationship with a woman.

HELP FOR THE HURTING

One of the important insights about sexual addiction is how easy it is for people in the addict's life to become dehumanized, as were the women in Warren's life. The addict is driven to have "it," and does not care with whom. The person with whom "it" is done is, above all else, an object for sexual satisfaction.

Partners of sexual addicts are not treated as human beings with needs and feelings but as fixes. Instead of sex being a healthy and nourishing experience with another person, sex is a craving that is to be satiated at almost any cost.

Some addicts' drive includes the need to victimize—that is, to hurt or to humiliate or to degrade another person. Rape is a sexual act that hurts; it is sex used as a weapon to destroy rather than as a tool to nourish. That is why rape is described as an act of violence and crime rather than as an act of passion. Rape is not the only sexual act that hurts others, however. Any sexual act that degrades, dehumanizes, or makes an object of another person is sexual victimization. Pornography is a prime example.

Male and female pornographic models and actors and actresses have names and needs and personal identities. They have probably been victimized repeatedly before they ever reached the pages or the screens of pornographic material. Then, they are overpowered into being used in pornography or submit to it because they find an identity in being used that way. The person who views pornography could care less about the subjects' identities. Instead, the addict "uses" the persons on the pages of the magazines or in the films as objects for sexual satisfaction—the addict victimizes the subjects.

If you or someone you care about seems to be locked into a sexual addiction, refer to chapters 23 and 24 for some recommendations of what to do. Sexual addiction needs to be courageously recognized, and help needs to be sought. Few sexual addicts are able to overcome the addiction by themselves. And they don't "grow out of it." Most sexual addicts have been sexually victimized or in some way sexualized in childhood. That's the level where the healing needs to take place.

SUMMARY

Certain sexual addictions are obvious to most folks: visits to prostitutes, use of pornography, and hopping in and out of bed with numerous sexual partners. Other sexual addictions that occur within marriages or as ways of dealing with emotional pain are not as obvious, though they are every bit as serious. All sexual addictions need to be confronted through counseling so that recovery can begin.

5

When What You Eat Starts Eating You

Food, A Common Addiction

To look at singer Karen Carpenter, you would have thought that her life reflected the lyrics of one of her best-selling records that proclaimed, "I'm on the top of the world, looking down on creation." She was pretty; she had a beautiful voice; she was a talented drummer; her walls were covered with gold records; she had earned tremendous amounts of money from her world tours and record sales. She had everything . . . except personal contentment. Slowly, she starved herself to death, a victim of anorexia.

Sometimes it takes the death of a celebrity to bring attention to a serious eating disorder or other addiction or compulsion. If you feel that you or someone you are concerned about may have an addiction to food or a related eating disorder, pause now to read the list below of twenty statements. Put a check mark before each statement that is true.

Is There an Eating Disorder?

❏ 1. This person has decided to stop overeating for a period of time but without permanent success.

❏ 2. There are people in this person's home who feel this person's eating is a problem.

❏ 3. There are people at this person's place of employment who feel this person has an eating problem.

❏ 4. People have suggested to this person that he or she has an eating problem.

❏ 5. This person's eating occurs on occasions of being angry or upset or as a way of trying to deal with worry or trouble.

❏ 6. The person takes refuge in eating from the troubles and people around him or her.

❏ 7. This person feels guilt or remorse about overeating.

❏ 8. Food and thoughts of food are controlling portions of this person's life.

❏ 9. This person has lied to others about how much he or she has eaten.

❏ 10. This person sometimes sincerely promises others that he or she will cut back on eating but without success.

❏ 11. This person eats in secret.

❏ 12. This person eats when bored.

❏ 13. This person eats when not hungry.

❏ 14. This person eats normally in front of other people and then makes up for it later.

❏ 15. This person hides food for personal use.

❏ 16. This person tends to starve himself or herself and grow very thin, but still thinks he or she is actually fat.

❏ 17. This person has gone on eating binges and then responded by vomiting, using laxatives or vigorous exercise to try to compensate.

❏ 18. This person's day seems to be measured by food more than anything else. Activities such as school and work are things to be endured while waiting for the next opportunity to eat.

❏ 19. This person has a reputation for trying fad diets from time to time but without permanent success.

❏ 20. There are particular times of the day when this person has cravings for food that are more out of habit than hunger.

If you marked any of these statements, we urge you to give some serious thought to what it means about this person's life. Obviously, the more statements you marked, the more it means there is a possibility of a problem and the need for some kind of professional evaluation to know for sure.

FOOD FOR THOUGHT

In *Diana: Her True Story* (New York: Simon & Schuster, 1992), Andrew Morton noted that so much media attention was focused constantly on Lady Diana Spencer after her 1980 engagement announcement to Prince Charles, she became abnormally conscious of her public image. She went on a radical diet and lost 14 pounds prior to her wedding in 1981. Morton writes that on the eve of her wedding, Diana "ate everything she could and then was promptly sick. The stress and the tension of the occasion were partly to blame, but the incident was also an early symptom of bulimia nervosa, the illness that took pernicious hold later that year . . . in fact, virtually from the moment she became Princess of Wales, Diana has suffered from bulimia nervosa which helps to explain her erratic dictary behavior."

If eating disorders can strike at Princess Diana, Karen Carpenter, actresses Jane Fonda and Ally Sheedy, gymnast Cathy Rigby, and many other celebrities who have shared their problems publicly about their eating disorders, these problems can hit anyone. Ironically, bulimia is a way for women under great stress to show some control in their lives. Perhaps they didn't have control as a child because they were ruled by a dominating, abusive father, so now they attempt to feel a sense of control by controlling their food ("I can eat when and what I want").

As we have noted with other addictions, the stereotypical image of the food addict does not fit the expected profile. Most people expect them to be fat. It is true that there is a correlation between being overweight and having a food addiction, but it is also true that there are many people who have food addictions who don't show it and are not overweight. This does not mean they do not have a dependency on food or that they are not using food as a way of dealing with emotional pain. It just means they are doing a better job of hiding their addiction.

Western civilization seems to idolize the perfect female body. A century or more ago, women who were overweight were envied because it meant they had been getting enough to eat, whereas many of the common folk were starving. In our current society, however, we have an abundance of food, so we admire people who are thin. For a fact, during the 1980s the drawings of the Campbell Soup Kids, which had always shown two chubby-cheeked "healthy" youngsters, were redrawn to reflect trimmer, leaner, more attractive children. Mothers today think of chubby kids as being overweight and unattractive.

EATING DISORDERS EXPLAINED

Judy Alley has been a counselor since 1982 at Alpha Counseling, specializing in helping patients who are dealing with eating disorders. Judy holds a B.A. in secondary education and an M.A. in psychology, and she is a licensed Marriage and Family Clinical Counselor.

"The eating disorders of anorexia and bulimia occur 95 percent of the time among females," says Judy. "It can start as young as ten years old. Sometimes women suffering from bulimia—in which they binge on food and then feel guilty for breaking their diet so they use laxatives or vomiting to expel the food—can disguise their addiction for many years. In time, however, they will develop serious problems of dental decay, gum disorders, and a ruptured esophagus from the poor nutrition and vomiting."

Judy says that typical bulimics are women with low self-esteem and a lack of confidence. They can often be childlike and moody, even irresponsible. Many of them enter professions where they can be caretakers (even nurses).

"Eating or losing weight is just a symptom of the real problem," says Judy. "These actions are a cry for help, even though at times it may be a silent cry for help. A place for recovery is needed. In my counseling I usually note strong emotional themes related to parental problems. One of my patients, a grown woman living on her own, told me, 'If my dad calls me and puts me in my place about something, I feel like throwing up. My dad shoves his philosophy of life down my throat, and I turn around and throw up until I get him out of my system.'"

Judy notes that many bulimics are so practiced at vomiting, they can mentally trigger a reflex that will cause spontaneous vomiting as many as eight times a day. They are truly addicted to this pattern of behavior as a way of life. They will sometimes even go to the edge of becoming violently ill but then will start to eat a little bit. This isn't because they want to put on weight; it's because they know that if they enter a hospital they will lose control over their lives, and they dread that more than anything.

"The anorexic patient is equally concerned with control," says Judy. "She continues to diet despite the fact that she is already abnormally thin. If I ask her, 'What area of your body do you hate?' this sort of woman will respond, 'Oh, I loathe this fat, flabby stomach of mine; I'd rather die than have this,' but, of course, she doesn't have a fat stomach."

Judy says anorexics exist primarily on fluids.

"I had one patient who only ate one meal per day," recalls Judy, "and it consisted of two thin slices of lean turkey and a small portion of fresh broccoli. The rest of the time she just sipped noncaloric diet drinks or water."

Judy notes that young girls who develop eating disorders often have similar problems. As a girl matures her body goes through some natural physical changes caused by hormones; if a girl is insecure about these changes, she isn't able to cope with them and she tries to counteract things by dieting. Other times the motivation to diet can come from peer group pressure or culture in general: the thin girls get to be cheerleaders and they have the boyfriends and they are the ones the parents like to brag about and show off. Another problem can stem from poor family dynamics, such as an insecure mom who is always dieting or who feels unsure of her husband's love; this insecurity can be sensed by the daughter and be picked up by her. Many women with eating disorders are victims of physical, emotional, or sexual abuse.

"Because of the way women are portrayed in magazine ads and television shows, girls begin to think that 'thin is in' and whatever you have to do to achieve that is okay," says Judy. "One in every ten girls will experiment with radical dieting and will stay with it to the point of addiction. That's serious."

To assist women in recovery from food addictions, Judy Alley has to supervise behavior retraining. She first explains to her patients what normal eating patterns are. She then starts her counseling at the point at which the woman's emotional problem has reached, whether it is dealing with a sense of being lost or it involves trying to cope with a major crisis in that woman's life.

Emotional exploration is done to try to discover what is missing in this person's life. The therapist is the platform in the transition from dependency to recovery. Once recovery begins, the food addict needs new challenges to meet and new things to comprehend. A focus on a different kind of control is created.

SIDE EFFECTS OF FOOD

It is important for food addicts to realize that even though they don't become inebriated from food, they actually can get a sort of "high" from food. Some people really have such a relationship with feelings associated with eating. Some people even have biological food sensitivities that literally can put them in a stupor after overeating.

We know, for example, that some people are allergic to certain foods. Everyone in the medical community recognizes the existence of allergies. But there also is a mysterious realm of food sensitivities. The point is, different people are affected in very different, significant, and often severe ways by food. If eating gets out of hand, whether for a biological or an emotional reason, it is prudent to seek professional help to recover from the disorder.

6

Tall Tales and Exaggerations

Habitual Lying

In one of the early episodes of the now-defunct "Newhart" television show, the innkeeper Dick Louden asked his neighbor Curt about a problem he was having with constantly lying.

"Is your problem with lying getting better?" asked Dick.

"Oh, yes, I'm practically cured of it," said Curt. Then after a short pause, he lowered his eyes and said, "Oh, no, there I go again."

Although meant as an attempt at humor, that little scene is very close to the truth. People who are habitual liars often want to be honest and sincere with their friends and family, but their fear of being rejected for saying the wrong thing is so strong, they concoct a "better" response. Although they mean well and they are desperate for acceptance, chronic liars are their own worst enemies. Their lying frequently makes them untrustworthy and deceitful in the eyes of other people. The lies and fabrications that were supposed to make the liar more acceptable can actually make him or her more unacceptable.

Do you know someone who lies and exaggerates and fabricates stories and situations? Do you wonder if you, personally, have a problem in this area? If so, pause now to read the list below of ten statements. Put a check mark before each statement that is true.

Is Lying a Problem in This Person's Life?

☐ 1. This person lies about "small" things, such as the ages of children when buying movie tickets.

☐ 2. This person lives in constant fear that his or her lying is going to be discovered.

☐ 3. Lying has done harm to an important relationship in this person's life.

☐ 4. This person has committed (or considered committing) an illegal or immoral act to cover up for a lie.

☐ 5. This person tells "little white lies," but then must tell bigger lies in order not to get caught.

☐ 6. This person feels guilty and remorseful about lying and promises to stop, but then continues to lie.

☐ 7. This person's lying has led to trouble with the law.

☐ 8. This person has lost a job or been denied a promotion because of his or her lying.

☐ 9. A professional person (pastor, physician, counselor) has told this person he or she has a problem with lying.

☐ 10. There are people in this person's family or at his or her place of employment who feel this person has a serious problem with uncontrollable lying.

This quiz is not meant to be a substitute for a complete analysis by a professional counselor or licensed therapist. It may, however, help you gain a new perspective on how severe this person's problem is with lying.

If you marked any of these questions, we urge you to put some serious thought into what it means about this person's life. Obviously, the more statements you marked, the more it means there is the possibility of a problem and the need for some kind of professional evaluation to know for sure.

THE PINOCCHIO SYNDROME

Children like to play "dress up" and to tell stories about their make-believe homes and spouses and babies. They like to get dad's tools and pretend they are "fixin' stuff." Society does not consider this to be lying. It's role playing and it's actually healthy. Kids see potential in themselves to one day grow up to be capable adults.

Conversely, when a child steals a piece of candy from the candy dish and then tells mother, "Uh-uh, I didn't take it," society frowns on that. In this second situation, the harm of the theft has been hidden by the deception of the lie. One wrong has been compounded by another. The child needs to be told in direct ways that lying is unacceptable for children *and* adults.

For a fact, thanks to lessons at home, at school, and at church, most children are provided with a clear understanding of the fact that lying is wrong. Why is it, then, that adults have a tendency to lie? There are several reasons we can cite: sometimes it is just a matter of what people consider to be self-protection (like telling the boss a report is just about ready when it actually hasn't been written yet); other times it might be related to vanity (like lying about one's age or the amount of salary you make); still other times it could be motivated by ambition (such as slandering a colleague in order to make yourself look better); or it may simply be rooted in fantasy (such as telling the women at the office that you've been going out with a great-looking guy who takes you to fancy places, when in reality you've been sitting at home each night watching sit-com reruns).

There's no denying that many people are circumstantial liars. Back them into a corner, and they will lie to get out of a situation. Some of these people, however, are chronic liars. Chronic liars are people who need things in their world to be different from what they are, so they lie about these things in order to disguise the hurting reality they cannot face. Chronic liars also are people who tell other people what they think those people want to hear.

Consider the situation of "Harry," a man who used to attend the church Rich Buhler pastored. Upon first getting to know Harry, you would never assume that he was telling you lies because everything he said sounded so truthful. He was divorced, living alone, and he liked to talk a lot about his former wife who had hurt him. He also had a four-year-old son.

Harry would come to church and talk about all the places he'd been to the week before. It made for fascinating stories because, to hear Harry tell it, he was a very successful "freelance artist." Sometimes he would play a song or two on the church organ and then tell everyone that he had earned a bachelor's degree in music from a well-known Bible college. He also sang in the church choir. Folks were impressed with his talents and his "credentials."

The odd thing about Harry was that you could never pin him down on anything about his past. People would say, "Hey, my brother went to that college too. Did you have any classes with a guy named Frank Jones?" To this, Harry would either respond by going into a long, rambling story that wound up having nothing to do with the question or he would act like he hadn't heard the question. Also, when people asked Harry where his freelance art work could be seen, he never gave a point blank response. It was always "in a nearby town." Before long, people began to suspect that Harry wasn't on the up and up.

The whole situation came to a head one day when Rich made a telephone call to Harry. It turned out that Harry had two separate phone lines running into his house: one was for personal calls and the other was for a very small, quite unsuccessful warehouse brokerage company Harry had started. When Rich called, Harry accidentally responded with his company name and thereby revealed that he wasn't an artist, he was a warehouse broker.

When Harry realized he'd been caught, he became so frustrated, he stopped the conversation and hung up the phone.

This warranted a face to face visit from Rich, at which time Harry broke down and confessed to his pastor that he wasn't a college graduate, wasn't a freelance artist, and wasn't an expert musician. Like all chronic liars, Harry tried to justify why he had been lying to everyone at the church, but Rich— firmly, yet kindly—convinced him he had a problem that needed to be treated with professional counseling.

During counseling, Harry revealed that he had been

abused by an emotionally and physically abusive father. Harry was brilliant, but his potential as a person had been broken by his father. It took a considerable amount of time for Harry to recover.

As with many other conditions, chronic lying is a way of dealing with deep pain and an effort to try to live as long as possible without having to face the painful truth. A chronic liar is a person who has had to create his or her own world in order to satisfy the need for the world to be the way he or she wants and needs it to be (as opposed to the way it really is). A chronic liar has developed that talent early in life and, sometimes, even believes his or her own lies.

SUMMARY

Lying is not uncommon among all children and adults. This is an unfortunate fact of life. However, chronic lying takes this common human flaw and transforms it into a way of life. Its purpose is to create an artificial world that will hide pain and make the liar seem more acceptable to himself and those around him. It is a weary life, however, and one that can be changed through proper counseling.

7

My Necklace Is Missing . . . Again

Stealing

"He got caught with his hand in the cookie jar."
"She's robbing Peter to pay Paul."
"Can I steal a moment of your time?"
"I filched a doughnut off the snack table."
"He'd steal pennies off a dead man's eyes."
"She pilfers note pads and pencils from the company all the time."
"They plundered that stock account as soon as their dad passed away."

Common expressions? You bet. And the implication? Simply this: part of our human make up seems to bend us to the act of stealing.

As children, one of the first words we learned was, "Mine!" We wanted to possess things. It came as a rude awakening to discover that mother did not always agree. "No, no," she'd say, as she pulled a toy away from our greedy little hands. "That belongs to your sister. Those are your toys over there. Leave this one alone." This would anger us. We'd pout and cry, but mother would not change her mind. Certain things were off limits.

This same lesson was underscored as we grew older. If we

snitched some candy from a store, our dads would take us to the manager, make us admit our misdeed, return the candy, and apologize. The manager, playing the part of the "heavy," would tell us how lucky we were to have a dad who was willing to teach us right from wrong. "If *I* had caught you," the manager would roar, "I would have called the police!" That scene stayed burned into our memories for a long time and worked wonders in keeping us honest.

In time, however, the old nature resurfaced. We began to "fudge a little" on our taxes but didn't consider it stealing since "it's *my* government anyway." We occasionally would "borrow" some money from the office coffee fund, but somehow would never get around to repaying it. We'd take company sample items home for our families to use because "the company has plenty of extras." We weren't really evil, we were just slippery.

Many of us, unfortunately, are this way. It's a constant battle of the will *not* to yield to theft. There is an old Arabian saying that warns, "Opportunity makes thieves." Or, as Oscar Wilde admitted, "I can resist anything except temptation." If theft is made easy, any one of us is capable of committing the act. Thankfully, although we are *capable* of stealing, we are also capable of *resisting* the desire. And that latter capability is the mark of a healthy adult.

Some of us, however, have become addicted to stealing. For some of us, stealing, in one form or another, has become habitual. In those cases, we need to call it what it is—an addiction. Then there is more of a likelihood that something can be done about it. Do you know someone who steals? Have you wondered about yourself in this regard? If you suspect that someone you are concerned about or perhaps you, personally, may have a problem with stealing, take a moment now to evaluate the statements below. Put a check mark before each statement that is true.

Does This Person Have a Problem with Stealing?

❑ 1. This person has stolen something for the purpose of giving the stolen item away as a gift.

☐ 2. This person lives with a fear of getting caught at stealing.
☐ 3. This person has repeatedly stolen small things from his or her place of employment.
☐ 4. This person has stolen during times of intense emotional pain.
☐ 5. Stealing has affected this person's reputation.
☐ 6. This person knowingly buys stolen goods at ridiculously low prices but feels innocent because he or she didn't personally steal the items.
☐ 7. This person has been caught stealing and has been reprimanded or arrested.
☐ 8. This person has willfully cheated an insurance company on a claim in order to bilk the company of more money.
☐ 9. This person has stolen things for the thrill of it.
☐ 10. This person loses sleep because of worries about having stolen something.

As always, we wish to caution you that this list of statements is not a substitute for a complete analysis by a competent therapist. It may provide some guidelines, however, that will help you determine whether you or someone you are concerned about needs professional counseling for a problem with theft.

If you marked any of these statements, we urge you to put some serious thought into what it means about this person's life. Obviously, the more statements you marked, the more it means there is a possibility of a problem and the need for some kind of professional evaluation to know for sure.

UNDERSTANDING THE URGE TO STEAL

The headline on March 28, 1988, was shocking to most Americans: "Bess Myerson Arrested for Shoplifting."

Shoplifting? Bess Myerson, Miss America of 1945 and famed consumer advocate? Naw! Impossible. Surely not.

Yet, there it was, with an arrest record and all. One of America's beauty queens, a fashion trendsetter, a spokeswoman for numerous corporations and associations, a contender for U.S. Senator from New York, and a self-made millionaire had been caught stealing small items from Hall's

Department Store. It seemed unbelievable. And what made it even more baffling was that the $44.07 worth of earrings, batteries, nail polish, and sandals she had stolen could easily have been paid for with the $160 the police found when they searched Myerson's purse after the arrest.

Earlier in the year Myerson had been photographed by a newspaper reporter as she removed andirons from the lawn of Nancy Capasso without the owner's permission. Ms. Capasso later accused Myerson of stealing the andirons and other items from the Capasso home (*Queen Bess* by Jennifer Preston, Chicago: Contemporary Books, 1990, pp. 275–6).

The public was stunned by these revelations. Why would someone as successful as Bess Myerson steal things? It seemed neither logical nor ethical nor practical . . . nor even needful.

Bess Myerson is not the only public personality to be caught at stealing. In his book *Poison Pen: An Unauthorized Biography of Kitty Kelly* (New York: Barricade Books, 1991), author and researcher George Carpozi revealed that Kitty Kelly has been accused of thefts and exposed as a thief numerous times. [Kitty Kelly's biographies of Frank Sinatra, Elizabeth Taylor, and Nancy Reagan have been bestsellers despite being panned viciously by reviewers.]

Carpozi reports that while in college, Kitty Kelly was caught by police when she stole items covered with dust that stained a thief's hands with a dye that showed up under ultraviolet light. Kelly was made to return money, clothes, jewelry, and a volume of Shakespeare she had stolen from other dorm rooms. She then was dismissed from college. Her sorority sisters also told Carpozi that whenever they took Kitty Kelly home with them for term breaks, their parents later called to say that numerous items were missing from their houses. In later years, Kelly was suspected of stealing a book manuscript from the home of author Barbara Howar, as well as other thefts.

But why, you may ask? Kitty Kelly was a beauty pageant queen as a teenager; she was a functionary in the Democratic Party during her twenties; she became a multi-millionaire through the sale of her books; her photo has been seen in most of the major newspapers and magazines in America. Why would someone that rich and famous and successful need to steal anything from anyone?

It just doesn't seem to make sense.

The problem is not limited to women either. In July, 1992, Marla Maples, the girlfriend of Donald Trump, reported that her press agent had been arrested because he had been videotaped stealing high-heeled shoes, combs, brushes, underwear, books, and photos from Marla's penthouse apartment in New York City. Upon searching the agent's office, police found many other stolen items, most of which were of no actual use to the man. The agent did not need the items; he just needed to steal. Ms. Maples told T.V. news reporters, "I just want him to get psychiatric help. He needs it."

These examples of successful, well-to-do people who were arrested for being chronic thieves demonstrate that drives to steal have nothing to do with an item's value or a person's need for that item. It is the act of stealing itself that is of primary value to the thief, for the theft provides a way of dealing with some emotional issues in life.

Chronic thieves are people who are trying to deal with a very painful world. They have deep pain, deep hurts. They are sometimes harboring great anger and feel the need to lash out in some destructive way. Sometimes there is a theme to their stealing—i.e, they consistently steal toys they were denied as a child, clothes they never were able to wear. Other times their stealing is just a response to a restrictive or victimized life. Still other times, it is strictly anger driven. Whatever the motive, the root lies in emotional injury.

To look at Bess Myerson, you would not think there could be any emotional injury in her life. Yet, there was plenty. She was the first Jewish girl to become Miss America, and she did it right at a time (1945) when Jews were being persecuted by the Nazis. She provided a rally banner for her people, but wearing that mantle of responsibility was a heavy burden. In later years she had one emotional shock after another: canceled television shows; three marriages that ended in divorce; a lost bid for the U.S. Senate; and a trip to court for an alleged tie to underworld mobsters. It seems to have broken her in the end. After she confessed ("under protest") to having shoplifted, one of her closest friends told reporters, "It was a cry for help! Bess *wanted* to get caught" (Preston, *Queen Bess*, p. 277).

Similarly, George Carpozi reported that Kitty Kelly was the daughter of an alcoholic mother who was always trying to dominate Kitty. Sooner or later, some sort of emotional backlash was inevitable. It was only a matter of time.

SEPARATING SYMPTOMS FROM INJURIES

One woman, whom we'll call Agatha, came for counseling when she realized that she could not visit anyone's home without stealing something from it. Although she had never been caught stealing or accused of stealing, she noticed that she was receiving fewer and fewer invitations from friends.

The items she had stolen had all been small, not overly expensive things, such as a miniature figurine, a transistor radio, a pen and pencil set, a paperback novel, and an ashtray.

Most of the items had no useful function for Agatha. She would later tell her counselor, "I kept most of the things hidden in my upstairs closet because if I put them on display or used them, my friends might spot them and realize I was the one who stole them."

Agatha, herself, was baffled by her drive to steal. She asked her counselor, "Since I believe that stealing is wrong and I have absolutely no use for the items I've been stealing, what is it that makes me do it?"

The counselor explained to Agatha that the stealing she was doing was only a symptom of a much greater problem buried within her. After many meetings with her therapist, Agatha discovered that when she was only seven she had experienced a great feeling of betrayal and abandonment when her mother ran off with another man. Agatha's father had compounded Agatha's emotional trauma when he vented the anger he felt for his wife on Agatha.

Agatha had grown up feeling abandoned and used and unloved and unworthy. This created both fear and anger in her, and her acts of stealing were ways of both striking back and nourishing herself when the emotional pain became too great for her to cope with. It was her way of responding to her emotional pain.

With counseling, Agatha made great strides toward recovery. Others like her have made similar progress.

SUMMARY

We learned in this chapter that a drive to steal is very similar to other addictions in that the act is only a symptom of the problem and not the problem itself. Habitual stealing is the response of a person who is deeply wounded. If the deep root of this person's emotional problem can be discovered and dealt with, the symptom (stealing) can be dealt with. Emotional recovery is the key.

8

You're Too Close to Me

Relationships That Stifle

The motion picture *Fatal Attraction* terrified, yet enthralled, audiences worldwide. The plot focused on a married man who had a brief affair with a woman who subsequently became obsessed with him. She called and visited him continually even though he tried to rebuff her. Finally, the woman became so consumed with the idea of securing a relationship with the man, she decided to eliminate any barriers holding her back. That meant killing the man's family. Her total determination to succeed at this made the movie's climax absolutely gripping.

Indeed, it is scary to think that one human being can become totally "addicted" to another human being. Nevertheless, it's not uncommon. Certainly, the extremism of a situation such as that in "Fatal Attraction" is not the norm in all cases of obsessive relationships. Still, such unhealthy relationships are detrimental at any stage or level.

Pause now to read the below list of eleven statements. Place a check mark in the space before each statement you feel applies to you (or to someone else you have a concern about in this area of relationship addictions).

Is This Relationship Addictive?

☐ 1. This person is so terrified of being alone, he or she will do almost anything to keep a relationship from ending.

☐ 2. This person seems willing to take more blame and carry more guilt in a relationship than is really his or hers to carry.

☐ 3. This person feels confined to making decisions or choices that only the other person in the relationship agrees with.

☐ 4. This person seems to be drawn into relationships with people who need "rescuing."

☐ 5. This person has a hard time saying no to the other person in this relationship.

☐ 6. This person has had more than one relationship that has turned out to be unhealthy or abusive.

☐ 7. This person has compromised personal standards or morals or has considered participating in illegal activities in order to preserve this relationship.

☐ 8. This person has considered ending an unhealthy relationship but has avoided it because of the fear that no other relationship might be available.

☐ 9. This person's friends and family have tried to warn him or her about unhealthy relationships but without much impact.

☐ 10. This person seems to be controlled by relationships and by the fear of losing relationships.

☐ 11. This person has lied or helped cover up for serious problems in the life of the other person in the relationship.

If you recognized yourself or someone else in the above list of statements and if you marked three or more, it is probably a good idea to get a professional evaluation as to whether addictive relationships have become a problem in your life or someone else's.

THE HUMAN OBSESSION

People enter into and remain in addictive relationships in a variety of ways. Gaylen Larson worked with a couple some years ago who had become so obsessed with one another, they had virtually isolated themselves from the rest of the world after fifteen years of marriage.

The husband, for example, commuted a long way to work.

There was a car pool from work and a van pool from his neighborhood he could have joined, but he preferred driving himself and being alone. The wife, for her part, stayed home and cooked, cleaned, and made crafts, but seldom ever had any guests or neighbors over. The husband would call his wife once or twice each day and she, in turn, would phone him a time or two. They just wanted to "say hello" and hear the other's voice. This clinging to one another not only isolated them from the world, it began to make them dysfunctional unless they were together. Through counseling, they were shown the value of having a broader base of friends and personal interests.

A related but different sort of addictive relationship is fostered by people who have a "rescue mentality." These people are addicted to unhealthy relationships with destructive people whom they feel they can help by giving faithful, sacrificial, all-enduring devotion. Of course, this does not work because the person supposedly being "rescued" only used this total devotion to exploit the "helper." There are many people who have a boyfriend or girlfriend to whom they are addicted in this manner. Some marriages are also like this. It's a very unhealthy relationship.

The term that is frequently used now to describe addictive relationships is *codependency. Codependency* describes an unhealthy dependence on another person. The wife of an alcoholic who lies and covers up for her husband and who prevents him from carrying the full weight of the responsibility for his addiction is codependent with him and with his problem. The parent who can never say no to a child and who seems unable to let that child increasingly carry responsibility for his or her own life is codependent with that child. The adult who lives irresponsibly and constantly relies on Mom or Dad or friends or co-workers for money or necessities of life and who cannot carry the burden of them himself is living codependently.

Bette Boyd is a counselor with Alpha Counseling who has spent many years working with codependent people who go from one addictive relationship to the next. Bette received B.A. and M.A. degrees in psychology and counseling from

California State University, Sacramento. She has been a licensed marriage and family clinical counselor since 1979.

"The codependent individual puts everyone else's needs before his or her own needs," explains Bette. "Normally, when someone provides love or help to another person as a gracious gesture, that is healthy. However, when a person devotes all of his or her life to someone else as a way of meeting a *personal* need, that is not healthy. This latter person is looking for a result that will meet an internal need. The need is insatiable because there is a great emotional injury with the person. As a result, this person becomes addicted to obsessive relationships because he or she is continually reaching out."

Bette says that the codependent person believes that if people, places, and things were only different, they'd feel loved and confident. So, by being faithful, the person hopes things will change. Naturally, it's an impossible situation. Nevertheless, the codependent goes on believing, "If I'm nice and accommodating, there's more likelihood that I'll be able to hold on to this special person in my life. And maybe things will get better."

The emotional injuries that can lead to the development of an obsessive relationship are numerous, but Bette Boyd notes some of the most common causes: (1) a trauma in early life; (2) parents who were physically and emotionally distant from children and, as a result, poor family bonding; (3) a sense of abandonment, sometimes intensified by "maintenance" child care; or (4) neglectful parents who did not attend to a child's needs or praise or encourage the child.

"We sometimes never realize how traumatic some of these factors and conditions can be," Bette emphasizes. "For example, I recently had a patient who was only five years old who was suffering greatly from feelings of abandonment. His daddy was an army reservist who had been called up for active duty unexpectedly. When he left, the little boy told his playmates that his father was dead. The little boy wouldn't let his mother out of his sight. His mother and I tried to explain to him that Daddy was away 'at work' and would be back. The boy wouldn't believe it because he knew that Daddy always came home each night from work. Finally, we had to set up a long-distance phone call and then an emergency leave. We felt it was that important."

Bette notes that other separations, such as divorcing, can be very hard on codependent people. Whereas some people see divorce as new freedom, codependents feel adrift on a boat on an ocean.

"When people come to us for counseling, we like to involve them in group sessions," says Bette. "This gives them a feeling of acceptance. When they talk, their ideas and feelings are validated by others. Our itinerary is simply to give them the strength to look into themselves, face the truth, and, ultimately, get to a point where they can say, 'I am willing to let go of harmful relationships.'"

SUMMARY

We saw in this chapter that there is a great deal of difference between a supportive, helpful, and caring person and someone who is a dominated, always-yielding, emotionally distraught individual. The codependent person who becomes addicted to unhealthy relationships has a deep emotional need that can never be met by doing results-oriented things for someone else. Only the discovery of the hurt within and the treatment of it through counseling will lead to recovery.

9

The Odds Are Not in Your Favor

An Addiction to Gambling

T he surest way to double your money is to fold it in half and put it back in your pocket.

Not all people believe this, as evidenced by the fact that state-run lotteries are able to offer contest payoffs as high as ten, fifteen, and twenty million dollars. A lot of people had to squander a lot of cash just to enable one person to walk off with the whole "pot."

The thought of being able to get rich quick drives many people to gamble with money they cannot afford to lose. Naturally, not everyone who takes an occasional chance on a state lottery is someone who is addicted to gambling, and, of course, people who *are* addicted to gambling would find other outlets if state lotteries were not so prevalent. However, there are many people who "play the odds" far more than is good for them. For them, gambling is a harmful aspect of their lives.

Do you think you know of someone who may fall into this category? Do you wonder if your own gambling practices might be becoming excessive, even addictive? If so, pause now to read the twenty statements listed below. Put a check mark before each statement you feel is true.

Is Gambling a Problem?

☐ 1. This person has decided to quit gambling but has been able to stop only for a limited time.

☐ 2. There are people in this person's family who feel that this person's gambling has become a problem.

☐ 3. There are people at this person's place of employment who feel this person has a gambling problem.

☐ 4. People have confronted this person about his or her problems with gambling.

☐ 5. This person has missed time from school or work because of an incident related to gambling.

☐ 6. This person has committed or has considered committing an illegal or immoral act because of gambling.

☐ 7. This person uses gambling as a way of coping with emotional pain.

☐ 8. This person feels guilt because of all the gambling.

☐ 9. This person has been arrested or threatened with arrest because of gambling activities.

☐ 10. Gambling is more important than protecting friendships to this person.

☐ 11. This person has lied because of gambling.

☐ 12. This person has been known to gamble in secret.

☐ 13. This person has promised his or her loved ones he or she will stop gambling, but the promise gets broken.

☐ 14. This person hopes that gambling will enable him or her to pay off debts and solve income problems.

☐ 15. After losing, this person feels he or she needs to start gambling again as soon as possible to try to make back the losses.

☐ 16. After winning, this person wants to gamble again to try to keep increasing the winning total.

☐ 17. This person has gambled until he or she has lost every bit of his or her available money.

☐ 18. This person believes that a certain portion of his or her money should be set aside for gambling and not be used for regular living expenses.

☐ 19. This person likes to celebrate good news by gambling.

☐ 20. This person's worries about gambling debts sometimes prevent him or her from relaxing or getting a good night's sleep.

Now, count up the number of check marks you made. While this little quiz can in no way be considered a proper substitute for a complete psychological and emotional analysis by a licensed therapist, it can help you discern whether a need for such help is apparent.

If you marked any of these questions, we urge you to put some serious thought into what it means about this person's life. Obviously, the more statements you marked, the more it means there is a possibility of a problem and the need for some kind of professional evaluation to know for sure.

YOU BET YOUR LIFE

Kenny Rogers has starred in three television movies in which he played the role of Brady Hawkes, a high-stakes gambler. These movies were spin-offs of a hit recording by Rogers called "The Gambler."

Television has always portrayed gamblers as romantic, heroic, steel-nerved individuals. Bret, Bart, and Brent Maverick were great gamblers of the Old West during television's 1950s. Likewise, Palladin and Bat Masterson were seen regularly playing at the poker table.

The silver screen has given us a long list of gambling movies, ranging from *The Cincinnati Kid* to *The Color of Money*. Gambling is always portrayed as something exciting, thrilling, and daring. For a fact, it is seldom any of that.

The reason gambling is so dangerous is because its victims don't really fit the Hollywood stereotypes. They are not the wealthy Diamond Jim Bradys nor the low-life hucksters milling around bookies. In all likelihood they are business people in your neighborhood, people you see at your office building, or maybe even members of your extended family.

Rich Buhler, when serving in pastoral counseling, dealt with people who had worked very hard to earn good lives for themselves. Some, however, after a gambling addiction took hold of them, lost their cars, home, savings accounts, and retirement funds. In what seemed a blinding flash, they had lost everything.

To understand why people become hooked on gambling, we first must understand that gambling is a unique addiction. Like all other addictions (drugs, alcohol, overeating), it is an activity someone gets involved in to help cope with pain. While gambling, the mind isn't concentrating on the other painful aspects of this person's life. Gambling can serve as an emotional anesthetic. A person experiences pleasure while acting out the addictive behavior.

Unlike other addictions, however, gambling is unique in that it offers at least a hope of something positive in the long run. Gambling might—just *might*—make someone a millionaire. Rational people realize the odds are ludicrous; but then, hurting people who are desperate for a way to ease their pain (gambling) *and* to justify their behavior (I could hit it big) aren't really rational.

What is also at issue here for many people is a matter of "eligibility." Simply put, if a person feels he is a loser, he will also assume that he is not eligible for anything good to happen to him. ("I am such an idiot. I'm such a loser.")

As such, this person will gamble his money in the hope that "fool luck" will not know of his stupidity and, therefore, may smile on him. At least it's worth a try . . . and, well, another try . . . and maybe one more try. Also, winning might mean, "I'm eligible."

NICE GUYS, HIDDEN ADDICTIONS

Mitchell was a nice guy. He was a family man and had no enemies. Mitchell did have trouble holding down a job. And he and his family suffered because he was so frequently unemployed. What Mitchell's family didn't know was that he had a secret addiction to gambling, which began when he was in the army.

"I had always been a privately tormented person," Mitchell said. "I felt like the black sheep of my family. I felt I was always having to live up to my brother's reputation and that my father didn't approve of me.

"Prior to joining the army, I'd never been exposed much to gambling. Then all of a sudden, I was always around it. We played poker, bet on baseball and football games, bet on who was going to get promotions. We bet on almost everything.

"I became hooked on it. It didn't matter whether I won or

lost, I just couldn't stop doing it. I don't know all the reasons; I just couldn't resist a good bet on a poker game."

Mitchell lost a large sum of money during his army days. It wasn't unusual for him to remain on base during a leave because he was broke from gambling. He didn't think much of it, though, because a lot of other soldiers lost money too.

After the service, Mitchell got married and tried to leave the gambling behind. He thought that it was just a part of his life in the army, and thus was no big deal.

One day, Mitchell discovered a racetrack that was about a forty-five minute drive from his house. There, he first experienced the thrill of betting on horses. He then made connections with illegal off-track betting, which extended beyond horses to other sports events.

"There were cities near me where gambling was legal and where some Las Vegas type games were available," Mitchell said. "But I knew I'd be risking my reputation if I went there so I never got into that. The secret betting, however, became addictive for me."

Predictably, Mitchell lost money—a lot of money. He used credit cards to their limits. He took out mortgages on his house. He sold valuable possessions, often saying they had been stolen.

Mitchell's wife began to discover the problem when she tried to find out where all the credit card money was going, then learned of the mortgages. Because Mitchell handled the finances, he had mangaged to keep the mortgages a secret. But one day a letter from one of the mortgage companies came in the mail and Mitchell's wife opened it. When she saw how much had been borrowed and the high monthly payments that had resulted, she panicked.

The crash for Mitchell came when he finally reached a state of bankruptcy. In desperation, he stole some merchandise from the manufacturing firm where he worked, and was caught.

Humiliated, Mitchell confessed to his employer what was going on. The firm agreed not to prosecute if Mitchell sought help and paid for the losses. Mitchell went into counseling and became active in a chapter of Gambler's Anonymous, a

12-Step program for gamblers that has helped thousands of people. Not only was Mitchell able to contain his gambling through his recovery but he was able to deal with the issues in his life that had fueled it.

People who gamble sometimes claim they can stop anytime they want. Some will even try to "prove it" in the most bizarre of ways. One man being counseled by Rich told him he was not addicted to gambling even though he had done it for years. He explained that whenever he felt the urge to gamble, he would draw out a specific amount of money, go to Las Vegas, and once he had lost all of that money he would stop. This behavior, he said, proved he had control over gambling and not vice versa.

"Have you ever come home with more money than you left with?" asked Rich.

"Well, no," admitted the man.

"Have you lost a lot of money over the years?"

"Only a flat one thousand dollars per summer trip," bragged the man.

"For how many summers?" asked Rich.

"Oh, about nine," the man calculated out loud.

"And you are trying to tell me that someone who has lost $9,000 on a clockwork schedule has no problem with gambling?" Rich said, pressing him.

The man paused, then answered, "Well, I guess when you add it all up it does look pretty bad. But if I would have ever hit the jackpot you wouldn't be talking to me like this."

"That's not the point," said Rich. "You *didn't* hit the jackpot. What you *did* do was lose $9,000 that could have helped pay off your house or secure your retirement. You played with fire and got burned so slowly, you didn't realize you had been fried."

Was this man addicted to gambling? Not in the typical sense. He was able to stop after he'd lost a certain amount of cash. To him, it was a form of recreation. Most of us might think that it was a waste of good money, but that's a value judgment, not a psychological assessment. An addiction to gambling would not have allowed the man to quit after losing just $1,000.

SUMMARY

We noted in this chapter that gambling is like all other addictions in that it is a way of escaping emotional pain, yet it is unlike other addictions in that it held out an elusive carrot that gave false hope of a wonderful outcome. We also noted that most people addicted to gambling (or even those who can be considered "problem" gamblers) do not fit stereotypes and, thus, may be hard to spot until it's too late.

We also discovered that some people who enjoy recreational gambling use limitations, such as "controlled" gambling, to protect themselves from getting into problems with gambling. Whereas these people may be spending their money in ways that most of us would not consider wise, they are, nevertheless, not necessarily addicted gamblers.

When the Going Gets Tough . . . The Tough Go Shopping

The Shopaholics We Love

You've seen the bumper stickers, haven't you? You know, "Buy 'til ya Fry" . . . "Shop Until You Drop" . . . "Y'Mall Come" . . . "I Came, I Saw, I Bought."

Those expressions can be considered cute until a few facts about excessive shopping are laid before you. By June of 1992, Visa and MasterCard reported that during the 1980s and 1990s, they had lost *five billion dollars* to "deadbeat clients." These were people who had bought things with a credit card but then were unable to pay off the credit card debt.

The opposite of that situation is just as bad in its own way. There are thousands of people with credit cards who pay only their minimum monthly payment and carry over the rest of the debt from month to month. On most bank-issued credit cards, this carry over debt is billed at 18–23 percent annual interest. As such, when honest people *do* pay off their credit card debt (with an income tax refund or Christmas bonus), they are spending hundreds of dollars just in interest fees.

Excessive shopping is a losing proposition no matter how you view it. People need to put limits and controls on their wants and desires. Some don't seem to be able to, however.

What about you? Have you ever wondered if your spending habits might be getting out of control? What about your spouse or your children? What about other people you care about? Do they have spending problems?

If you suspect this may be true, pause now to respond to the list of twenty statements below. Put a check mark in the space in front of the statement if you feel it is true of the person you have in mind.

Is There an Addiction to Spending?

☐ 1. This person will decide to stop overspending for a time but then will revert to the old habits.

☐ 2. There are people in this person's family who feel this person has a serious problem with spending.

☐ 3. People have tried to convince this person that he or she has a spending and shopping problem.

☐ 4. This person has committed or considered committing an illegal act because of a problem with overspending.

☐ 5. This person has borrowed money or sold personal items in order to solve problems incurred by overspending.

☐ 6. This person's method of coping with anger and frustration is to go into stores and spend money.

☐ 7. This person goes out shopping as a way of not having to be around other family members or friends.

☐ 8. This person feels tremendous guilt and grief after going on a needless shopping spree.

☐ 9. Shopping is beginning to consume a major portion of time in this person's life.

☐ 10. This person has been known to go on a shopping spree but return everything for refunds in 30 days.

☐ 11. This person has lied and covered up about spending.

☐ 12. This person has made promises to stop spending money uncontrollably, but has broken the promises.

☐ 13. This person will go shopping secretly.

☐ 14. This person has changed addresses or switched phone numbers in an attempt to escape bill collectors.

☐ 15. This person has given false information on forms in order to secure extra credit cards.

☐ 16. This person loses sleep because of shopping indebtedness.
☐ 17. This person will buy sale items even when unneeded.
☐ 18. This person has borrowed money from one credit institution just to help satisfy other creditors.
☐ 19. This person often runs his or her credit cards to the maximum limit.
☐ 20. This person is terrified of being put on a budget.

Now, as always, we want to explain that this quiz is not meant to be a substitute for a psychological and emotional analysis by a licensed therapist. Its purpose is merely to help you discern whether or not professional help may be needed to deal with the problem.

If you marked one or more statements, we urge you to put some thought into what it means about this person's life.

Obviously, the more statements you marked, the more it means there is the possibility of a problem and the need for some kind of professional evaluation to know for sure.

I'LL BUY AWAY, O GLORY!

The addictive shopper feels like he or she has to shop. The bumper sticker reads, "In the Sweet Buy and Buy." Shopping shields addicts from the hurts of life. Addicts may have been wounded in one or more ways—either through sexual abuse, emotional abuse, or physical abuse. Their shopping, especially for clothes, temporarily makes them feel good about themselves.

In our work as counselors we have seen shoppers display their habits in several ways. One sort of person in this category is the "bulimic shopper." This person will go out and buy things on a binge, gobbling up all sorts of storefront items. It feels good. It creates a feeling of control and self-fulfillment. A week or two later, however, this same person will become overwhelmed by guilt about how much money he has spent. Frantically, he will rush around the house and put all of the items back into their boxes and bags. He'll then spend the day going from store to store returning the goods and asking for his money back.

Returning the goods for a refund, however, is not evidence of a change in this person's life. At some later time, when the emotional pain from which this person is suffering starts to resurface, this person will once again go on another shopping binge. Like the bulimic eater who gorges on food and then induces vomiting to purge the stomach, the bulimic shopper will repeat the shop-and-exchange procedure over and over.

Some people observing this behavior might say, "Just stop them from doing that. Freeze their checking accounts. Take away their credit cards. Limit them to a cash allowance." Such actions would only be responding to the symptom of excessive shopping and would not be focusing on the emotional pain that is motivating the activity of shopping. Without proper counseling to discover and mend the real injury, complete recovery is very difficult. Cutting up credit cards would only create more anxiety, not heal the emotional wounds.

Another person in this category is the "secret shopper." This person knows that excessive shopping can be damaging to the family budget, but she just can't control herself. She feels compelled to shop. So, she does it deceptively. She will shop, but she will not make it obvious to other members of the family what she has bought. Additionally, she will hide the credit card bills from her husband so that he won't be aware of the excessive spending. She may even have five or six credit cards for stores, gas stations, phone companies, and other retailers that her husband doesn't know about.

Naturally, deceptions like this cannot go on forever. No matter how cleverly the shopper hides the bills, sooner or later it catches up to her when more money is being spent than is being earned.

Again, the treatment for this action should not only be a limiting of credit card accessibility (although from a pragmatic stance that may, indeed, be necessary). That would be controlling the spending, but it wouldn't by itself lead to healing.

You see, when true healing takes place, the addictive behaviors aren't just suppressed or replaced by others. Even the desire for the addiction can be eased. For this to happen, one must look at where the need for escape comes from. People must deal directly with the problem rather than just the symptom. An addiction such as excessive shopping is a symptom of something that is out of balance in a person's life.

An addiction is much like a weed growing in a garden. The garden starts out fresh and clean. The dirt is rich and ready for planting. Beautiful flowers are planted there, and it looks as though this garden will be a beautiful showpiece. Then the winds of adversity blow and a weed seed is blown in from a neighboring field and dropped onto the fertile soil. The seed sends down its roots and, before long, it is growing strong. The weed begins to choke out the beautiful flowers that were growing there, and it takes control of the garden. The gardener comes along and sees this ugly intruder and tries to pull it out, but it is deeply rooted and it won't budge. He must clean up the garden, so he gathers up all his strength and pulls very hard.

The weed snaps and the top of the weed, the visual part, comes off.

Now the garden looks clean and the gardener is happy.

However, the roots are still firmly planted, and before long the weed springs up again. It grows strong and soon it takes over the entire garden again.

The only way to get rid of the weed permanently is to get at its roots. This is true of an addiction to shopping too. Take away a credit card or checkbook, and you've just cut off the top of the weed. The root (the emotional injury) is still present in the person. It must be reached, through counseling, before the behavior can be changed.

SUMMARY

Spending restraint is necessary for all of us. For the addicted shopper the shopping sprees provide a way of controlling one's life and dulling the pain. Until this person can enter into recovery, the "root" of the injury will probably not be discovered and dealt with.

Planes, Trains, and Automobiles

Hobbies and Recreational Activities that Run Amuck

A story is told of two golfers who were on the putting green of the seventh hole. A ways away on the highway a funeral procession was passing by. One of the golfers paused, put his hat over his heart, and stood reverently until the hearse had passed.

Noticing this, the other golfer said, "My, that was certainly a gracious and respectful thing for you to do."

"It's the least I could do," said the first golfer, as he replaced his hat and started to line up his putt. "Next week we would've been married twenty-two years."

That makes for a pretty funny story until you pause long enough to think about someone you know who is just about that avid when it comes to golf or some other hobby or recreational activity. The fascination may be stamps, baseball cards, antiques, rare books, horses, camping, poker, the guitar, classic cars, sports, autographs, woodworking, or even lawn care. The point is, when a pastime becomes excessive, it can create problems.

What about you? Have you ever wondered whether the

amounts of time and money you devote to an avocation or amusement are healthy or unhealthy? Have you ever wondered those same thoughts about a fad or hobby being pursued by your spouse or someone else you care about? If so, please read the list of statements below and put a check mark before each statement that is true.

Are This Person's Hobbies Excessive?

☐ 1. This person's involvement with a hobby or recreational activity has resulted in neglect to family and friends.

☐ 2. This person has taken unauthorized time off from school or work or has skipped other commitments in order to pursue a favorite pastime.

☐ 3. This person has spent money needed for family support on things related to a hobby or recreational event.

☐ 4. This person retreats into the world of his or her hobby whenever troubles confront him or her.

☐ 5. This person has stolen things for use in his or her hobby.

☐ 6. This person seems to have a feeling of self-worth only when he or she is involved in the hobby or recreational activity.

☐ 7. This person's hobby or recreational activity is capable of endangering his or her life.

☐ 8. This person's conversation is dominated by talk about his or her hobby or recreational events.

☐ 9. This person's job performance is not consistent because he or she daydreams too much about a hobby or recreational activity.

☐ 10. This person subscribes to vast numbers of magazines that he or she can neither afford nor has time to read.

The preceding test is not meant to serve as a substitute for a complete analysis by a licensed therapist, but rather just as a tool for helping you discern whether a potential problem exists or not.

If you marked any of these statements, we urge you to put some serious thought into what it means about this person's life. Obviously, the more statements you marked, the more it means there is the possibility of a problem and the need for some kind of professional evaluation to know for sure.

RIDING THE HOBBY HORSE

A hobby can be a very positive part of a person's life if it serves to get the hobbyist's mind off the stresses and strains of other pressuring factors, such as work loads and poor health. However, when a healthy interest in a pastime becomes an addiction, it can be a detriment to the hobbyist's normal life and to those people around him or her.

People who have addictions may go through several basic stages. It is helpful to understand these stages. The first stage is when the activity provides a distraction from the emotions or feelings related to pain. Like other addictions, a bondage to hobbies can be a part of a pattern of escaping pain or the responsibilities of life.

Rich Buhler once worked with a man who was well known for his hobby of model trains. His entire basement was filled with an enormous train set and it had been beautifully put together. The man had every reason to be proud of it. What most folks who admired the set didn't realize was that for the owner it was more than just a leisure time interest. It was an addiction. He spent virtually every free moment either working on the trains, attending meetings of the train club he was a member of, or hanging around with other train enthusiasts. His wife felt abandoned, and his two sons spent very little time with their father and, interestingly enough, had little access to his precious trains. They were the envy of other kids in the neighborhood because of their father's trains, and yet they benefited little from it.

This man was filled with pain and didn't feel able to communicate with his wife or to include his children in his hobby. Few people knew it, but he was also an alcoholic. His basement was a world where he was in control and the orderliness that he hungered for could be accomplished. He was a perfectionist with his trains and he hungered for the recognition his train layout secured for him. It could also be said, however, that in a tragic way his basement was his life, at least the part of his life that he felt okay about. His commitment to what could otherwise be a great hobby that could include his children instead became an interference with his family and other areas of his life.

The second stage is when the obsession becomes progressive. One man whom Gaylen counseled had become interested in classic cars after he'd inherited a 1937 Hudson from his grandfather. At first, the man spent his weekends working on the car; however, as the car began to look nicer and nicer and the man started getting more and more compliments about his work on it, he began to spend his weeknights working on it too. Soon, every spare moment the man had was spent working on that car.

This man had never received much positive reinforcement in life. His parents had doted on an older brother of his. He never seemed to measure up to all the older boy's accomplishments, and that experience left him feeling inadequate. Then, later in life when he started to receive compliments about his work on the classic car, he became obsessed with the idea of finally being "the best" at something. It dominated his every waking moment, to the detriment of his job, family, and friendships. Finally, with everything falling apart around him, the man sought counseling about his addictive hobby.

There are two additional stages of a developing addiction. One is when the activity begins to alter the person's mood. It has an actual tranquilizing effect and helps dull the feeling of the pain that person is escaping.

Another stage in the addiction occurs when the person spends a disproportionate amount of time either thinking about the activity or actually being involved in it.

SUMMARY

Hobbies and recreational activities should be a nourishing part of a healthy life, and many of us need to pursue them. When they become a refuge from some of the difficult realities of life, however, and a substitute for healthy relationships or when they begin to interfere with more important priorities, such as family or job or health or finances, we need to ask ourselves, "Why?"

The Biceps Tell It All

When Exercise and Self-improvement Become a Bondage

Any American who has a desire to keep fit will not lack for ways to do so. Health clubs, racquetball clubs, and swimming clubs are found in most cities. Aerobics shows are broadcast every day on television. Home video workout tapes by Richard Simmons, Jane Fonda, Debbie Reynolds, Angela Lansbury, and numerous other celebrities are on sale nationwide at very reasonable rates.

Television commercials abound that show gadgets "guaranteed" to trim your thighs, tighten your buttocks, flatten your stomach, tone your muscles, and shape your legs. People can purchase home workout equipment ranging from rowing machines to stationary bicycles and from weight benches to treadmills.

Keeping in shape has physical appeal and medical benefits. When the routine of working out each day becomes an obsession, however, it can ultimately do more harm than good.

If you are concerned that a member of your family or someone you care about or you, yourself, may be indulging in excessive exercise, pause now to take the quiz below. Put a check mark in front of each statement you feel is true of the person you have in mind.

Is Exercise Becoming a Problem?

☐ 1. There are people in this person's home who consider his or her commitment to exercise or self-improvement to be out of balance and, thus, a problem.

☐ 2. This person has gotten into financial trouble because of the amount of money or time spent on exercising or self-improvement.

☐ 3. This person is never satisfied at his or her levels of athletic achievement or exercise conditioning or accomplishments.

☐ 4. This person takes refuge in exercise or self-improvement from the troubles around him or her.

☐ 5. The exercise is controlling portions of this person's life (schedules, vacations, work shifts).

☐ 6. This person feels crushing guilt and a sense of failure if he or she misses a day of exercise.

☐ 7. This person has experienced medical problems due to the intensity and frequency of exercise.

☐ 8. This person has been late for work or has missed work due to unswerving loyalty to exercise or self-improvement.

☐ 9. The involvement in exercise or self-improvement has interfered with family events and other important functions.

☐ 10. This person's circle of friends seems to be mainly people who are equally devoted to exercise or self-improvement.

As in all the previous chapters, we wish to caution you that this test is not a substitute for a complete physical examination by a physician or a complete analysis by a licensed therapist. However, it will provide some parameters for your evaluation of the situation.

If you marked one or more statements, we urge you to put some serious thought into what it means about this person's life. Obviously, the more statements you marked, the more it means there is the possibility of a problem and the need for some kind of professional evaluation to know for sure.

PHYSICALLY FIT TO KILL

The word "addiction" sounds so strong. It brings to mind images of a bum sleeping on a sidewalk of a big city with a brown-bagged bottle clutched in his hand, or of a drug dealer making a deal in a dark alley. Certainly, these are true reflections of *some* addicts. What some of us may not realize, however, is that the opposite extremes of behavior can also be examples of addictions. People who only eat a strict, limited diet can be addicted to nutritional fads. People who run, train, and exercise non-stop can also be addicted to a need for physical perfection or the activity of exercise.

Famed body builder Charles Atlas, who developed an exercise regime called isometrics, often told audiences that the reason he became so muscular and strong was because as a child he had been bullied by bigger kids. Then one day, while visiting the zoo, he noticed that the lion was able to maintain its strength and form even while being caged. This was because it pushed its foreleg muscles against its backleg muscles in a series of push-and-resist exercises. This muscle against muscle technique became the secret of Charles Atlas's isometric training. He stayed at it night and day until he was so strong he could attach a rope to a locomotive and pull it down the track from a dead standstill.

Exercise became a total way of life for Charles Atlas. Recalling his painful embarrassment at the hands of bullies as a child, he developed a cartoon advertisement that recreated a scene of a bully kicking sand into the face of a skinny boy. This ad ran for many years in dozens of national magazines and helped to sell thousands of Charles Atlas body building courses. Apparently the same pain and humiliation Atlas experienced was something being experienced by many other boys and men. The pain of embarrassment and humiliation sometimes lead to an obsession with exercise.

RUN FOR YOUR DEATH

People develop exercise obsessions for many different reasons. One of the most common reasons is *compensation*. A woman who feels her face is not pretty may try to develop a voluptuous body as compensation. A man who is short or who has gone prematurely bald may try to prove he is still as virile as the next guy by building up his muscles. A high school boy with poor academic grades may compensate by throwing the shot put farther than anyone else. A young woman in college may not have as much money as her sorority sisters, so she constantly diets and exercises in order to make the other girls envy her great figure.

Compensating is a way of coping with a poor self-esteem. If the individual feels he or she is not good enough for some reason, exercise becomes a tangible way of trying to even the score. Of course, it's a losing battle because it does not solve the problem that instigated the original need: a short muscular man is no taller than a short flabby man; a plain-looking woman looks just as plain whether she has a curvy body or an overweight body. Since the real problem never gets corrected (or properly adjusted to), the compensating continues to be an obsession. It's an endless cycle.

Another reason for addictive exercising is *escapism*. When the body is so focused on doing two hundred laps in a swimming pool or so focused on completing a twenty-six-mile marathon, it has neither the energy nor the capability of being distracted by negative thoughts. Roberta was a good example of this sort of person. She was a runner, and she committed herself to it with extraordinary effort. She ran more than six miles a day, usually in the morning, and regularly worked out at the local health spa to keep her muscles working as fit as her cardiovascular system.

Most of Roberta's friends and co-workers admired her. She was not only a great-looking woman who was obviously in top shape physically, but her running had become part of her identity. She would be the brunt of friendly jokes from other, out of shape, employees.

It was stunning, then, when the news was spread one day that Roberta had tried to commit suicide. She had overdosed on pills, and if her sister Joan had not walked into her apartment when she did and called for paramedics, Roberta would probably have died.

As a part of trying to deal with her own emotions, Joan went to Rich Buhler for pastoral counseling. There she laid out the story of Roberta's life and some of the insight that helped reveal that her running was not the healthy commitment others thought it to be.

"She's tried to keep up the charade that she's a physical enthusiast," Joan said, "but if you knew her eating habits, you'd know that she was not as concerned about her health as you might imagine."

Joan said that after Roberta had been admitted to a hospital following her overdose, she had been diagnosed as having an eating disorder. Roberta was terrified of getting fat and, for her, the running was a part of trying to ensure that it would never happen to her. She ate very little, and when she did eat, she would consume only a small variety of foods. Her concern about her body, including the eating and the exercising, almost consumed her.

Not surprisingly, Joan said, it was also revealed that Roberta had been molested when she was a child, and her counselors were helping her enter into recovery from that, as well as the conditions of an eating disorder and addictive running and exercise that had resulted. Roberta had not repressed the memories of being molested, but she had buried them, vowing never to tell anyone about what had happened. Until getting help, she never realized that she had an addiction and didn't connect any of her activities with the fact that she had experienced emotional injury in her childhood.

SELF-IMPROVEMENT ADDICTIONS

Other kinds of self-improvement can also become addictive. There are many people who have committed vast amounts of time and resources to schooling, attending seminars, buying books and cassette tapes or signing up for specialized training classes; yet these people never really seem to accomplish much in their lives. They'll read hundreds of books, collect dozens of diplomas or certificates of completion, or even hold several degrees before somebody realizes that the activity of self-improvement for these people is actually an addiction, a way of doing the same thing that an alcoholic does, only instead of drinking they are studying; and instead of getting drunk, they're getting intoxicated with activity that distracts from their emotional pain.

Rich Buhler had lunch one day with an acquaintance who

talked about his coming to realize that he was addicted to activities that never really seemed to produce the kind of self-improvement for which he had searched. This man had seven legitimate, earned graduate degrees from respected universities (including two in Europe). Interestingly enough, two of the degrees—a master's and a Ph.D.—were in psychology. His wife, however, got tired of always being married to a student. She grew disillusioned over the fact that her husband never seemed to get a steady job, so she left him.

The pain of that separation prompted the man to start re-evaluating his life. He came to realize that there was an enormous emotional hole in his heart from having grown up in a home where there was severe neglect and that he had been, on the one hand, trying to fill that hole with all his accomplishments, while, on the other hand, failing to do what was necessary to have a healthy relationship with his wife and failing to support his home adequately.

SUMMARY

Exercise and self-improvement can be healthy and should be a part of every life. There is no limit to the number of ways they can be pursued and with good effect. However, when they become an addiction to the point of dominating and controlling a person's life (even at the expense of other important priorities such as family), many problems can result.

The Accepted Addiction

Workaholism

As far back as the writings of the Apostle Paul, the rule of survival in society has been, "if anyone will not work, neither let him eat" (2 Thess. 3:10 NASB). Captain John Smith made this the rule when he set up one of the first colonies in America, and it has remained a firm part of the American work ethic ever since.

Of late, however, some people have begun to question the validity of a life that is absolutely dominated by work. Is it really as noble as we once thought? Is it really as necessary as it once was back during a time when the land was raw and times demanded that one work or die?

If you've ever wondered whether you or someone you care about has become a workaholic, pause now to respond to the following set of statements. Put a check mark in front of each statement you feel is generally true about the person in question.

Is This Person Addicted to Work?

☐ 1. This person has tried to balance his or her life by working less but without permanent success.

☐ 2. There are people in this person's home who consider his or her intensity or time spent with work to be a problem.

☐ 3. There are people at this person's job who have said this person works too hard and needs to slow down.

☐ 4. When people comment that this individual works too hard, he or she secretly feels good about being identified as an extremely hard-working person.

☐ 5. This person has experienced interruptions in important family priorities or family events because of always needing to be committed to work.

☐ 6. This person has committed or has considered committing an illegal or immoral act because of something that "must" be accomplished for work.

☐ 7. This person takes refuge in his or her work from the troubles and people around him or her.

☐ 8. Work is controlling this person's life.

☐ 9. This person conceals some of his or her work in order not to be criticized by family or co-workers about working too hard.

☐ 10. This person has health problems that could be the result of or aggravated by an addiction to work.

☐ 11. The people who are important to this person sometimes feel as though they are paying the price for this person's addiction to work.

☐ 12. This person seems to consider "things" more important than people.

☐ 13. This person lacks a sense of value or worth apart from activity related to work.

☐ 14. This person would have a hard time finding a reason to go on living if his or her work came to an end.

☐ 15. This person has a difficult time taking vacations or planning any leisure time.

☐ 16. This person talks about personal dreams he or she would like to fulfill one day, yet never gets around to that because there's too much work to do.

☐ 17. This person came from a home where a father or mother considered life to be all work and virtually nothing else.

☐ 18. This person finds value in other people only in relation to the work they can do.

☐ 19. This person brings a lot of work home from the office.

☐ 20. This person's spouse and children feel that they are less important to this person than his or her work is.

Now, let's take a moment to consider your responses. We do not want you to consider this twenty-statement list to be a substitute for a complete physical examination by a physician or a psychological analysis by a licensed therapist; however, looking at your responses may help you decide whether you or someone you care about needs to take this next step.

If you marked any of these statements, we urge you to put some serious thought into what it means about this person's life. Obviously, the more statements you marked, the more it means there is the possibility of a problem and the need for some kind of professional evaluation to know for sure.

Some workaholics often give the appearance of being someone who is always running around like a chicken with its head cut off. There's a flurry of activity and feathers are flying, but very little achievement is being noted . . . at least, not much in comparison to the amount of energy being put forth. This kind of workaholic has seven projects going on at once and he or she is always dashing from one to the next—a consultation here, a meeting there; an appointment here, a power lunch there. Busy, busy, busy. There's lots of work, but very few job completions.

There is a method ruling this chaos, however. There may be emotional pain there. And any activity this person can do instead of feel that pain seems a preferable action. If continuous work subdues the pain or pushes it away for a time, then work becomes an addiction.

Consider the example of Jean, the administrator of a small private elementary school in the Midwest. She is fifty-four years old and has been a licensed teacher for thirty-two years. She is very petite, attractive, and vivacious, as well as self-confident in all outward appearances. The school board appointed Jean as interim administrator after the previous administrator resigned unexpectedly. Jean had no credentials or experience in administration, but she leaped into the job with such exuberance, she was awarded the position at the end of her one year of interim status.

Jean virtually lives at the school. She arrives at 6:30 each morning and does a walk-through inspection of her teachers' rooms, leaving notes about anything that does not meet her standards. At 7:30 she holds a staff meeting where she gives announcements, asks about classroom needs, and then leads in a morning devotional time. From 8:00 until noon, she teaches a morning session of kindergarten. At noon she covers the office while the school secretary goes to lunch.

From 1:00 until 3:00 Jean answers phone calls, meets with parents, reviews curriculum texts, helps to plan fundraising events, assists with playground and recess duty, orders school supplies, and does dozens of other administrative duties. Once the students and teachers have left at 3:00, Jean goes to her classroom and prepares lesson plans, changes her bulletin boards, cleans the room, and gets things ready for the morning.

At 5:00 P.M. Jean drives across town in time to teach a 6:00 P.M. course in "Theory of Elementary Education" at a local college. The class ends at 10:00 P.M., but Jean stays to discuss term projects with several students. She arrives home at 11:15 P.M. She goes through the day's mail, listens to her phone answering machine messages, fixes a sack lunch for herself for the next day, works on cleaning the house a bit, then falls into bed around 1:30 A.M. She's back up at 5:00 A.M.

People warn Jean that she needs to slow down and take some time off, but she insists there's always too much that needs to be done. Even during the summer, she is actively organizing events to give her school more visibility as a way of increasing enrollment.

Earlier in her life, Jean had been a much different person. She had married the captain of the college basketball team, had settled into a beautiful new home in a classy neighborhood, and had landed a plum job as the hostess of a daily television children's educational show. Her husband became the principal of one of the big public schools. When they discovered they could not have children of their own, they adopted a baby. Life seemed perfect.

Jean and her husband Jim weren't much for saving or investing. Jean liked to buy nice things for her home and Jim liked sports equipment. Jim's job provided basic medical coverage and a basic retirement plan, so the couple left it at that.

Jean loved her work on TV. She was recognized all over town. Children sent her dozens of fan letters each week. She was in demand as a guest speaker for PTA meetings, church socials, and media events. She thrived on the popularity.

Then, in the 1960s, with the advent of sophisticated nationally syndicated children's shows such as "Sesame Street" and "Mister Rogers' Neighborhood," Jean's local TV show was canceled. She was stunned and heartbroken. In one flick of the switch, the limelight was turned off of her. The fan mail stopped, the speaking engagement offers dried up, and the local fame began to fade.

Being known locally for her work with children, Jean found it easy to secure a job as a kindergarten teacher at a private school. The work was fun, but not as glamorous as television. At the same time, two other unexpected events occurred. Jean's husband developed Parkinson's Disease and had to go on total disability. Also, Jean's father, who lived in town, suffered a stroke that left him 70 percent paralyzed and wheelchair bound.

Everyone expected Jean to leave her job and divide her time between nursing her husband and nursing her father. Jean felt trapped. Her perfect life had become a nightmare. She couldn't bear the thought of spending the rest of her life as a nursemaid to two invalids.

Then, suddenly, an opportunity presented itself. Her school's administrator resigned out of the blue and the school board needed a replacement *fast*. Jean raced forward to volunteer her services. She convinced them that with her name recognition, she could do wonders for school recruitment. At the TV station she had produced her own show, so she had supervision experience. Since it was only temporary, until a qualified person could be hired, the board agreed to give Jean a try.

Jean told her mother and her married sister that she needed to land this job because of Jim's medical expenses. This seemed convincing. The mother and sister helped care for the father and Jim.

As Jim's conditioned worsened, Jean spent more and more time away from him, first by earning a master's degree and then by getting a job teaching night school at a college. She used the work to escape the pain of life—her lost TV career, her invalid father, her sick and unemployed husband. At school, as the administrator, she again had control, respect, prestige, and freedom from "distasteful" responsibilities. Her workaholism was a buffer between herself and life's painful disappointments.

Regrettably, Jean's workaholism proved costly. The adopted son became embittered at the way he and other relatives were left by Jean to cope with the husband's daily medical problems. The son left home right after high school graduation and never came back. Jean's personal appearance showed the effects of long days, lack of sleep, and continuous stress. The lines in her face became very creased; her hair went gray; her voice became raspy and strained; her energy level ebbed very low.

As Jean's workaholism took its toll, her job performance became very substandard. The school board put her on probation and asked for several measures of accountability that Jean found difficult to achieve. Her life became a crossfire of agony: she still hated to be at home, but now she also felt inadequate at work. When she recently came in for counseling, it was obvious that she was greatly in need of help.

THE CINDERELLA ILLUSION

Jean's behavior is not unique. Many other people have behaved the same way under similar circumstances, says Linda Meferd, a psychiatric mental health nurse with Alpha Counseling.

"Workaholism is often something a person under great stress will manifest as a way of escaping the feeling of being trapped," says Linda. "Many people still have a bit of the Cinderella illusion in them. They want life to be 'happily ever after.' When something goes wrong, such as a divorce or the death or illness of a spouse, people experience the death of their dream. It's traumatic and scary."

Linda says that women and men need self-esteem "tools" to help them overcome workaholism. They must know how to establish their personal worth. Sometimes it is by learning to balance home and job responsibilities. Other times it is by learning to make choices, to manage crises, to set goals, and to accept responsibility.

Overcoming workaholism also frequently requires counseling. Behind the symptom of workaholism can be an emotional injury. For Jean, it was a loss of career and self-esteem when her TV show was canceled. For someone else, it might be a childhood incident of sexual molestation that left the individual with a need to "work up to" a level of self-worth again. For another person, it may have been the emotional trauma of living with an abusive parent who criticized but never approved of the person's accomplishments; as such, this person continues to work hard to do something— anything —that will be of value in that parent's eyes.

Through counseling, the hurting individual may be able to discover the cause of the emotional pain in his or her life. When that is found, it will provide great insights into why the individual has become a workaholic and what steps then can be taken to overcome this obsession with work.

Putting God First

Religious Addictions in the Lives of the Faithful

Rich Buhler has spent several years as a pastor, and he has seen problems of religious addiction. He has talked with other pastors who also recognize this problem in their churches. At first thought, it would seem that a person could never be too devoted to the work of the Lord; nevertheless, even Jesus left off from His healing and teaching and went away to spend time in a garden or in the wilderness or in a fishing boat. If a person has a balanced life in which dedication to church service is part of a weekly routine, this can be spiritually rewarding. However, if a person uses church work as a way of avoiding other responsibilities of home, family, or job or as a way of avoiding pain, this is neither healthy for the individual nor pleasing to God.

Rich Buhler was aware of a family in which the wife was very well educated, very self-confident, and highly admired in her church. She was the mother of five children, but she spent very little time with them. This woman was a good leader and could be counted on to make important church projects really "work."

To look at this woman on Sunday morning with her five children and her attractive appearance, you would automatically take her to be the epitome of a Christian spouse and mother. What most people did not know, however, was that her children felt neglected, her home was out of control, and her codependent husband was actually being more of a homemaker than she was (and he was very angry about it).

This woman was getting virtually all of her emotional nourishment from her involvement at church. She was there for every service and a lot of other events during the week. It was at the expense of her marriage and her children, however. Whenever her husband tried to tell her about how bad the situation was, the wife became defensive and angry. She accused him of trying to sabotage her work for the Lord.

The situation took on a whole new perspective, however, when the oldest child (an eleven-year-old daughter) developed cancer. The girl's condition required the mother to stay home more and to interact with the father in providing care for the daughter. Although the mother loved her daughter, it was agony for her to miss church worship services, committee meetings, and other church-related functions. She missed the praise she always received for her work, and it actually caused her to become angry with God because He wouldn't allow her to continue with her "church things."

This woman was forced to work things out with her husband and children. She had grown up in a home where both parents were achievement oriented, and that is why her church achievements had been critical to her. She eventually was able to learn that, while there's nothing wrong with a healthy commitment to the church, such work must not be done for the escape of dealing with pain or at the expense of important priorities of health and home.

Do you know someone like this woman? How about you, yourself? Have you or someone you know become so caught up in the busy activities of a church, you've lost perspective on everything else in life? Pause now to respond to the ten statements below. Put a check mark in front of each statement you feel is correct about the person you have in mind.

Is There a Religious Addiction?

☐ 1. This person has given power to a religious leader or a religious group to make decisions for him or her.

☐ 2. This person gives money to a religious organization that this person cannot afford to give.

☐ 3. If this person is involved in normal leisure activity, he or she feels guilty because no work is being done for the church.

☐ 4. This person seems to put religious activities on a higher level than meeting the needs of the family.

☐ 5. This person is critical of anyone who is not as loyal to religious activities as he or she is.

☐ 6. If this person has to miss a scheduled religious service for any reason (even illness), he or she has tremendous feelings of guilt.

☐ 7. There are people in this person's family or with whom this person works who feel this person's involvement with a religious organization has become a problem.

☐ 8. This person's family has suffered financially because this person has a preoccupation with religion and a belief that "making money" is not spiritual.

☐ 9. This person uses involvement with a religious organization to escape other responsibilities in life.

☐ 10. This person condemns and withdraws from friends and family who do not embrace this person's church.

Now, count up the number of check marks you made. While this little quiz can in no way be considered a proper substitute for a complete psychological and emotional analysis by a licensed therapist, it can help you discern whether a need for such help is apparent.

If you marked any of these questions, we urge you to put some serious thought into what it means about this person's life. Obviously, the more statements you marked, the more it means there is the possibility of a problem and the need for some kind of professional evaluation to know for sure.

RELIGION GONE AWRY

At this point you might be scratching your head and wondering how anyone can do too much for God. For a fact, we can't do too much for God, but we *can* do too much for the rituals and practices of organized religions. Let us give you an example straight from the pages of your newspaper. The events we are about to relate are bizarre, yet completely true.

On January 5, 1989, an unemployed truck driver named Larry Cottam and his wife Leona were arrested for murder in Wilkes-Barre, Pennsylvania. They were held in the Luzerne County Prison without bail. The murder victim in this crime was Eric Cottam, the couple's fourteen-year-old son. The cause of death was officially cited as starvation, but the more obvious cause was a misunderstanding of the Bible.

Eric Cottam was five-feet-ten, yet he weighed only sixty-nine pounds at the time of his death. He had not eaten any food for the last three weeks of his life because his parents refused to accept charity. They forbade Eric and his twelve-year-old sister, Laura, to eat free meals at school. They refused to apply for welfare checks or food stamps or loans or charitable grants. They insisted that God would miraculously meet their needs as He saw fit. It took Eric's death to bring them to their senses, but by then it was too late.

"I don't hold God responsible," Larry Cottam told reporters. "The error was on my part, not God's."

How true. How sad. How tragic. How unnecessary.

Younger sister Laura did not die, but she was diagnosed by hospital physicians to be suffering seriously from vitamin deficiencies, dehydration, and general malnutrition. Mr. and Mrs. Cottam told investigating police officers that they had not eaten food from November 22, 1988, to January 5, 1989. They were treated at Mercy Hospital in Wilkes-Barre before being taken to jail.

The ultimate irony of this true story is that besides being a truck driver, Larry Cottam was also an ordained minister. Furthermore, at the time his son starved to death, the Cottams owned two $50 U.S. Savings Bonds and had $2,131 in cash at home, $263 in a checking account, and $1,281 in an interest-earning passbook savings account! The Cottams told Pennsylvania State Trooper James J. Henry, Jr., that they couldn't use any of that money because it had been set aside as tithes and offerings for God, and as such it did not belong to them.

Truly, it is an odd twisting of logic for Christians to say on one hand that God owns the cattle on a thousand hills and that as a child of God those riches are the inheritance of all believers, and then on the other hand to say that money set aside for God cannot be used to save the life of a dying child. That is worse than inaccurate—it's criminal.

Correale F. Stevens, the District Attorney in Wilkes-Barre, said that the religious interpretations of Mr. and Mrs. Cottam were not adequate defenses for what they did to their boy. Said Stevens, "A son has died as the result of his parents' failure to provide him with the necessary life in terms of food, sustenance, and support."

The Cottam family's story is a tale of religion gone awry. These individuals made themselves victims of rules, regulations, and customs devised by man, not God. The Apostle Paul (see Rom. 14:1–10, Col. 2:16–23) preached against this sort of short-sightedness.

BUT DOESN'T GOD COME FIRST?

In his years as a pastor and family counselor, Rich Buhler used a simple exercise to help people addicted to church activities gain a better perspective on their lives. He would ask the person being counseled to make a list of priorities in life. Most people would have something like this: (1) God; (2) spouse; (3) children; (4) health; (5) church; (6) job; (7) service to the community; (8) hobbies . . . and so on.

Rich would then say, "You listed God first."

"Oh, yes," the person would say proudly. "God always comes first in my life."

"Does that mean that once you've done something God-honoring each day, you then can cross off God and move to the next thing on your list?"

The person would look shocked. "Why, no! I wouldn't cross off God. How ridiculous to suggest such a thing."

"The way you've arranged this, however," Rich would continue, "makes God in competition with your spouse and your children and it seems to restrict what you're doing for him as only being related to certain activities."

"What would you do?" asked the woman.

"God is first in my life," Rich replied, "but I don't actually put him on my list of things to do. God is the *reason* for my priorities and when I am serving my wife and children, it is part of my service for him. Also, instead of just putting God at the top of the list, I try to list some of the activities that I regard as 'ministry' so I can fit those into my other priorities."

Rich pointed out that a lot of people who put God at the top of a priority list tend to think that, as a result, church and Sunday school are at the top of the list as well. That is how church activities, themselves, sometimes displace spouse and family as commitments.

Because a religious addiction, like other addictions, can become a place to retreat when in pain, it is very easy for church or religious activities to become something that feels more like bondage than the freedom they are supposed to offer.

It takes honesty and discernment to know the difference between a healthy commitment to God and a tormented addiction to religious activity. Something that makes that even more difficult is the fact that some churches are pastored by people who are addicts and who require their people to be virtual addicts in order to be members in good standing. Recognizing that and taking steps toward health requires real courage. Jesus described some of the unhealthy religious leaders of his day as placing "heavy loads" on people's shoulders and yet not "lifting a finger" to help them. That's a good picture of an organization that is being ruled or influenced by addictive attitudes.

Jesus had compassion for people who were in that kind of suffering and said, "Come to me all who are weary and heavy-laden, and I will give you rest" (Matt. 11:28 NASB). He was talking to people who were beaten down and discouraged by what the religious leaders were requiring of them. "Take my yoke upon you, and learn from Me," Jesus said, "for I am gentle and humble in heart, and you shall find rest for your souls. For My yoke is easy and My load is light" (Matt. 11:29–30 NASB). In other words, in contrast to the demanding and abusive leaders that had required such unhealthy commitment from the people, Jesus is a person who will be a breath of fresh air in our desire to serve God and who will give us assignments that will not be burdensome and too heavy to bear.

Let us be voices that will encourage every person to respond to what we believe is a natural hunger in the heart of man to respond to God. Take steps toward trusting Jesus Christ and who he claimed to be. Knowing God and serving God will be the most enriching and fulfilling experience of life. Just be careful not to make it an unhealthy addiction or to be caught up in organizations that are, essentially, based on addiction.

PART TWO:

Emotional Volcanoes

Feelings That Commonly Underlie Addictions

Wasn't Grandpa Hot-Headed Too?

When Anger Gets Out-of-Hand

The fact that the Bible advises, "Be angry and do not sin" (Eph. 4:26) seems to indicate that anger can have its positive as well as negative side. Recent events in the news prove this. When one woman lost two children in accidents caused by drunk drivers, her anger drove her to form M.A.D.D. (Mothers Against Drunk Drivers). This was positive anger. Conversely, when Bernard Goetz became angry over gang members harassing subway riders in New York, he took a gun and shot four youths. This was negative anger.

Our language has developed numerous expressions to describe angry people: "He has a short fuse" . . . "She has a hairpin trigger on her emotions" . . . "He's constantly going around with a chip on his shoulder" . . . "She can pick a fight at the drop of a hat" . . . "He's hot-tempered" . . . "She's got a real mean streak" . . . "He stays ticked off all the time." The list is endless, for anger seems to be one of the most commonly recognized human emotions.

As we'll note in this chapter, anger can be channeled or redirected or deflected when handled by a person who is aware of what triggers it. However, when left to compound, anger can lead to violence, insults, or emotional distress.

Perhaps you have wondered whether the bouts of anger you've seen occur in someone's life (or perhaps your own life) are normal and acceptable. Take the following test and gain a perspective on that situation. Put a check mark in front of every statement that is true.

Is This Person's Anger a Problem?

☐ 1. This person's anger has resulted in physical harm to another person.

☐ 2. This person's anger has resulted in a job suspension, a demotion, or a loss of employment.

☐ 3. This person's anger has caused an economic loss for the person and for his or her family.

☐ 4. This person uses outbursts of anger as a threatening way of controlling and manipulating other people.

☐ 5. This person's anger, when displayed in public places, causes embarrassment to friends or family.

☐ 6. This person's anger has resulted in destruction of property or personal possessions.

☐ 7. This person's anger makes people afraid to share their honest thoughts and feelings with this individual.

☐ 8. This person's anger has caused alienation among his or her family members.

☐ 9. This person's anger has escalated to the point of needing police intervention to restore calm.

☐ 10. This person may not explode in anger, but he or she nevertheless has a way of making "someone pay" for creating anger in this person.

As we have emphasized in each previous chapter, this test is neither all-inclusive nor professionally conclusive of a person's mental or emotional condition. Only a licensed therapist or counselor can assess that on a one-to-one basis.

If you marked any of these questions, we urge you to put some serious thought into what it means about this person's life. Obviously, the more statements you marked, the more it means there is a possibility of a problem and the need for some kind of professional evaluation to know for sure.

THE EFFECTS OF ANGER

Everybody gets angry. As we've already mentioned, not every event of anger means that something is wrong or that there is a problem. Anger that causes destruction in the life of the person who has gotten angry or in the lives of those around him or to property is anger that has become a problem. The person expressing such anger needs to seek help for this.

While pastoring a church, Rich was contacted by a woman we'll call Michelle, who came to him for marriage counseling.

"I'm at the end of my rope," Michelle told Rich. "My husband and I have been married for nearly twenty years, but I've never felt more hopeless about our marriage."

Michelle was angry with her husband, but mostly angry with herself. She felt her anger was the reason her marriage was not working. And she felt this way because her husband, Rex, told her so!

As Rich looked into some of what was happening in Michelle and Rex's home, he realized that Rex was an angry and abusive person. Rex had convinced each member of his family that they were responsible for his anger.

"I've realized," Michelle told Rich after months of counseling, "that Rex is angry all of the time. He doesn't always show it, especially to people outside of the family. But I can tell it's always there.

"He can become irritated or blow up without warning. We all have been living in almost constant fear of his anger. Just last week, he got mad at our dog and kicked the poor animal halfway across our family room. I had to take it to the vet because it was in so much pain. It turned out the dog had suffered serious internal injuries, and it cost a bundle to get the dog treated. When I got home and told Rex how much the treatment cost, he blew up again."

When he wasn't angry, Rex had a winning personality, and he was very ambitious with his work. But his anger affected almost everyone he knew.

"He's gotten into a lot of trouble at work," Michelle related. "He supervises about ten people, and he abuses all of them with his anger. He pounds the desk when something isn't done at exactly the time or in the exact way he wants. He's been known to write abusive letters and memos to his workers. They walk on eggshells around him."

Michelle began to share her concerns with Rex, boldly, and suggested he get help. Rex was unusual in that he listened the first time Michelle confronted him and went for counseling. He joined a support group for abusive men where he learned that anger and abusiveness in his childhood home had contributed to his own rage. He had always thought that his anger was caused by all the stupid people he had to contend with each day at the office and at home. He had never thought he might be the one needing help and improvement.

PARENTAL ANGER

Many people grow up in angry homes. If a child is always being yelled at by a parent, the child comes to believe the treatment is deserved. He does not realize that the problem is the parent's uncontrollable anger and not any fault of his own.

As a result, the child thinks, "I'm always doing stupid things. I get yelled at because I'm continually messing things up. I never do anything right. I've just *got* to try harder to please my folks. If I do, they'll finally be happy with me and won't have to scream and holler at me."

This, of course, is an incorrect assessment of the circumstances. The child behaves better and better, but the parent continues to be angry. As a result, the child grows up feeling he is inherently bad or useless. Eventually, when this person learns that the problem was not his inadequacies but his parent's anger, he is surprised. How tragic to have lived so many years not understanding this.

Jill was an example of this. Her father was a fanatic about control and orderliness at home. Everything had to be organized, clean, and in its proper place at all times. Being a child, Jill was sometimes forgetful of procedures. If she failed to clear away her supper dishes after eating or forgot to hang up her school clothes or didn't remember to take off her shoes before entering the house, her father would rant and rave about it. He insulted her intelligence, called her hurtful names, and berated her as a person. Jill lived in constant terror of provoking her father's wrath.

Later, as an adult, Jill had such a low opinion of herself, she could not sustain long-term relationships with people and she bounced from job to job. She sought counseling to see if a therapist could help her with "her" problem.

The counselor helped Jill investigate her childhood. With information she obtained from her mother, other relatives, and people who had known her father, Jill discovered that her father had spent his life in a dead-end job that he hated. He had been pressured into working at his father's appliance store (although his dream had been to be a forest ranger in Montana). Jill's grandfather made all the business decisions at the store and allowed Jill's father no control over the employees, the finances, the advertising, or the general management.

Jill's father felt like a little child who could never be trusted to carry his own lunch money. This angered him to the point of outrage, but since he was too intimidated by his father's power to confront him, he instead directed his bitterness toward Jill. If he had no control over anything at the store, then, by heaven, he'd sure have control over *everything* in his home!

Once Jill came to understand the source of her father's continual anger and his fanatical need for control, she began to see that she had not been a terrible child, but really quite normal. This gave her a new perspective on herself as an adult. She was able to shed her negative emotional baggage and lead a more positive life.

VIOLENT ANGER

Although Jill's father did great damage to her emotionally and psychologically, he never physically hurt her. That is not always the case, however, with people who harbor great anger.

Lori sought counseling when she discovered that her husband of eight years was having an affair with one of her dearest friends. At her first counseling session, all Lori could do was moan, sob, and cry. She was so deeply hurt, she couldn't even talk. The second and third sessions were the same way. Lori would come for her appointment, but her entire time was spent wiping tears, blowing her nose, and shaking her head in bewilderment.

This situation created a sense of anxiety in the counselor, for he knew that in time all of this deep pain and sense of betrayal would regenerate in Lori as anger. And, the greater the initial pain, the more intense the eventual anger would be. He tried to give Lori some "homework" assignments to help her begin immediately to ease her pain and ward off the impending retaliation of anger. But Lori was too distraught to cooperate.

Then, suddenly, the change occurred. At Lori's fourth counseling session, she came in red-faced and resentful. She launched into a tirade against her husband that was so vicious and so continuous, the counselor couldn't get a word in edgewise.

"Okay, so maybe I'm not a sex queen," Lori said loudly, as she paced the office, "but I'm not frigid either. I met Alan's needs. He didn't have to shack up with my floozy friend Carla. Those lousy, double-crossing, two-timing back-stabbers! I hate them both. I'd like to scratch her eyes out. I'd like to get a knife and cut out Alan's lying tongue and then cut out his black heart. I cleaned his house . . . cooked his meals . . . paid our bills . . . ironed his shirts. And for the past six months, he's been making it with Carla! I don't deserve this. If I had a gun, I'd kill *both* of them!"

The therapist knew this process would occur; however, he had hoped to have time to set some safe guidelines for placing this anger within limitations. Lori's deepest sense of trust had been violated, resulting in tremendous hurt and the resultant anger. Her sense of life's orderliness had been upended and it had made her disoriented. Her feelings of love had been betrayed and she was left with a broken heart. All these emotionally devastating experiences had then united in feelings of hurt and loss. When hurt is not processed appropriately, the result is anger.

Anger can be directed inwardly or outwardly. If it is directed inwardly, a person like Lori will say, "His affair is *my* fault. I must be a bad wife." She may add, "I shouldn't have put on so much weight and I should have kept the house cleaner and I should have tried to be a much more interesting person. If I had paid more attention to my husband's needs, he never would have had this affair." These sort of inwardly directed self-criticisms result in feelings of depression.

If, on the other hand, anger is directed outward, a person like Lori will tell everyone, "My husband is a real jerk! I gave that clown the best years of my life. I was his cook and housekeeper and lover and the mother of his children, and the reward I got for all that devotion was a two-timing spouse!"

When a person directs anger inward, it causes the person to suffer (depression, sadness, a sense of failure). When a person directs anger outward, it causes everyone around that person to suffer (yelling, complaining, rampages).

The counselor tried to reason with Lori, but she would have none of it. She left the office as worked up as she had been when she had arrived. Maybe worse. She got into her big Cadillac and sped off toward home.

En route home, Lori saw Alan coming down the highway in the opposite direction. He was driving a mini-pickup with a hard plastic shell over the truck bed. In an instant, Alan became the target of Lori's wrath. She swung her car in a U-turn over the highway median. The cement curbs tore off her car's muffler and popped off a hubcap, but that didn't impede Lori's mission. She pressed the accelerator to the floor and aimed her car directly ahead at Alan's little pickup.

Alan spotted Lori in the rear view mirror. He took an exit ramp and tried to lose Lori amidst the side streets of a subdivision. That proved to be an unwise decision. When Alan turned into a cul-de-sac, Lori pursued him to the end of the street. She rammed the front of her big Cadillac at full speed into the side of Alan's pickup. The impact drove the truck up into a yard and totaled both vehicles. Alan and Lori both had to be taken to a hospital by ambulance, and Lori was subsequently charged with speeding, making an illegal U-turn, reckless driving, vehicular assault, and a long list of other offenses.

CONTROLLING ANGER

Not surprisingly, once Lori was calmed down again and she "came to her senses," she was appalled by her behavior. She couldn't believe that a rational, law-abiding person like herself could have behaved so violently out of control. She had *never* acted that way before in her life.

What her therapist had to explain to her in subsequent counseling sessions was that Lori had no skills for coping with anger. For most of her life it hadn't mattered, since nothing had ever caused her to feel the kind of anger she had felt about the affair her husband had had with her best friend. However, once her level of anger exceeded her ability to cope with it, Lori lost control and reacted instinctively and emotionally rather than rationally and logically.

Linda Meferd deals with patients and clients who are trying to cope with uncontrollable anger in their lives. Linda holds a B.S. in nursing and is a registered nurse. She also has a master's degree in nursing with a specialization in psychiatric mental health, and she is certified as a clinical nurse specialist. In her capacity as Director of Nursing for Alpha Counseling Centers, she both trains nurses and counsels patients herself.

"Some of the people who have come to me for counseling have been so angry, they have behaved like caged animals," says Linda. "One young man leaped from his chair and tried to smash his fist through a window. When left unchecked, anger can escalate to that level. It can become a very serious condition."

Linda explains that a counselor must first try to assess the depth of a person's anger.

"I must ask myself if this person is safe," she says. "Will this person hurt himself or herself or possibly hurt someone else? If I feel that this is a very real possibility, then I may recommend medication, possible hospitalization, or perhaps a stay at a live-in treatment center."

She adds, "Most of the time, however, I can offer help through counseling visits wherein I can teach the individual ways to recognize the symptoms of rising anger and how to deal with it."

Among Linda's many excellent suggestions for dealing with anger are the following specific ideas.

Recognize anger as it develops. One woman had been angry for many years over the fact that her husband paid so much attention to sports and so little attention to her. Unbeknownst to even herself, she had begun to vent this anger in cruel ways. When the evening sports announcer would begin to give scores on the television, the wife would choose that exact time to turn on the garbage disposal. When Monday night football games were televised, the wife always planned a late dinner so that her husband would miss the kick-off. These are examples of what is known as passive-aggressive anger, in that the expressions of anger seem mild and unintentional, yet they are done with deliberate forethought.

Finally, when the husband quit coming home until after he had seen the game at a friend's house or at a local bar, the wife sought counseling. The counselor showed her how her hidden anger had made her do things that had driven her husband away from home. The wife was amazed. She thought that because she never yelled at her husband, she had her anger under control. Not so, however. She was exhibiting what is known as passive-aggressive anger.

Provide a physical release for anger. When her patients meet with her, Linda Meferd often hands them a ball of modeling clay and tells them to squeeze the clay as they talk about things that make them angry. As emotions run high, the patients grip and mash and squash and pull apart the clay. Pent-up anger and anxiety are diffused this way, and a more constructive conversation ensues.

"If a patient calls me and tells me she is entering a stage of uncontrollable anger and she needs immediate counseling," says Linda, "I tell the patient to sit with a pillow in her lap and the phone cradled on her shoulder. As she talks to me by phone and I counsel her, she is encouraged to punch the pillow every minute or so as a way of releasing tension and aggressive feelings."

According to Linda, anger is like hot steam in a kettle: it has to have a blow-off valve or else it will explode.

Create a calming atmosphere. It has been said that "music doth soothe the savage breast" (not beast, as it is often misquoted). For many people this is true. People who are angry about a situation at work have found it helpful to play relaxing music on the way to and from work.

Soft pastel colors on office or home walls produce a sense of ease that bold red, brash orange, or solid black cannot generate. Phones and doorbells can be reduced several decibels to make their ringing less jarring. They can even be unplugged. There are a variety of ways that day-to-day annoyances can be reduced or eliminated.

Channel negative anger into positive work. One television actress was asked how she stayed so fit and trim. She responded, "It really angers me to read a negative review of one of my TV shows or movies. My blood pressure rises and I see red. That's when I grab my cassette player, turn up the volume, and spend thirty minutes doing aerobics. The workout not only keeps me in good physical shape, but it also allows me to get the anger out of my system. I benefit two ways."

Similarly, a professional football player has said, "If I get angry at myself for messing up during a game, I don't go home and kick my expensive furniture. No way! I go out on the field and kick the football. It drains my anger and improves my playing."

Get adequate rest. Some people become "short tempered" when they don't get enough sleep. Going to bed a little earlier or taking a mid-afternoon nap can be very helpful to such people.

Seek to confront the source of the anger. There are numerous reasons why people should seek the source of their anger. First, as we have learned in this chapter with the example of Jill, sometimes people can discover they are the victims of *someone else's* anger. This is very revealing. Second, as in the case of the woman who hated sports, people can be misdirecting their anger. This woman was really angry about not getting the attention and possibly the affection she felt she deserved from her husband. She felt neglected. She believed, "He thinks more about sports and television than he does of me." She was afraid to direct her anger directly at her husband for he might reject her even more, so she made the television the target of her displays of anger. As we noted before, she was showing passive-aggressive behavior.

SUMMARY

Linda Meferd says that life is a series of incidents— "snapshots," as she likes to call them. Some incidents evoke a harsh response from us. They make us *angry*. If our righteous anger causes us to take positive steps to change a situation, then our anger has been a motivating source for good. If, however, our violent anger causes us to lose rational control of ourselves and to cause harm, then anger has been a destructive force.

"Look for the best options," says Linda. "We all need a light at the end of the tunnel. Instead of always looking back at painful snapshots, take a look forward and ask, 'What is my next snapshot going to be of?' Choose something that will bring out your best, not your worst. Anger can be very self-destructive, as well as harmful to others. Since most of it is self-generated, most of it can also be self-diffused."

16

It's All My Fault

Guilt That Stands in the Way of Life

If you walk into a courtroom and look at the scales of justice, you'll see that they are held by a woman who is blindfolded. Her symbolic duty is to weigh the evidence and not be influenced by the appearance of the person who stands before her. If the evidence tips the scales one way, the suspect is innocent. If, however, the evidence tips the scales the other way, the suspect is guilty. It's that easy. Cut and dried. Simple and direct.

Such a succinct system of justice makes for great dramas. Everyone loves it when Perry Mason makes the accuser break down on the witness stand and admit that the defendant is really innocent. Ah-ha! Justice prevails and the guilty are punished and the innocent are freed.

Yes, in the world of TV shows and mystery novels, everything about guilt and innocence is clear cut and obvious. Unfortunately, in real life things are not often as distinct and delineated as they are in the world of fiction. In real life, there are people whom society has labeled "innocent" who nevertheless believe they are "guilty." Just *what* they are guilty of can range from the trivial to the monumental, but in each case the weight of guilt is always overwhelming.

What about you or someone you know? Is there a situation of carryover guilt that seems to be oppressive and emotionally injurious? Maybe you suspect this, but you are not sure. If so, take a few moments to complete the following short test. Place a check mark before each statement that you believe is true.

Is This Person's Guilt a Problem?

☐ 1. This person's life seems to be characterized by guilt.

☐ 2. This person has a hard time accepting honors or even receiving compliments.

☐ 3. People tell this person he or she seems to have a problem with feeling too guilty.

☐ 4. This person is immobilized or greatly hindered by feelings of guilt.

☐ 5. This person apologizes continually, even for little things.

☐ 6. This person feels that impending punishment or loss is always right around the corner.

☐ 7. This person feels too guilty to ever say no, and as a result has agreed to commitments that he or she really does not want to be involved in.

☐ 8. This person always feels so "sorry" for the way things are and feels personally responsible.

☐ 9. This person will sabotage a relationship or default at winning something because there is a feeling of guilt about having the good things in life.

☐ 10. This person is trapped in an unhealthy relationship because he or she would feel guilty about ending it.

As always, we caution you that this quiz is not meant to be a substitute for a complete psychological and emotional analysis by a licensed counselor or therapist. It may, however, give you an element of perspective on the guilt problems being faced by you or someone you are concerned about.

If you marked one or more statements, we urge you to put some serious thought into what it means about this person's life. Obviously, the more statements you marked, the more it means there is the possibility of a problem and the need for some kind of professional evaluation to know for sure.

THE GUILT COMPLEX

Rich Buhler knew a woman who in every way except one seemed as totally normal as a person could be. She was married, the mother of four children, active in her church and neighborhood events, and a person who was very pleasant to everyone she came in contact with. The one thing about her that was so distinctive was that she seemed to be living in constant guilt. As Rich recalls it, "She was guilt, itself, going somewhere to happen."

Every aspect of this woman's behavior seemed to ooze guilt. When she phoned people, guilt could be heard in her voice: "Hello, this is Julie . . . you probably don't even remember me . . . our kids go to the same school . . . and I'm really, terribly sorry to bother you . . . I know you're probably very busy and don't need someone like me to interrupt you . . . but I've been asked to contact parents about the field trip . . . ."

Her voice, her body language, her behavior, all telegraphed messages that indicated here was a woman heavily burdened by guilt. Then one summer she came across a copy of Rich's book *Pain and Pretending* and she found a vivid description of herself in that book. Reading the pages caused flashbacks of memory for Julie. In those memories were recollections of times of incest with her father. Although she had suppressed the memory of all that for many years, the shame and guilt it caused in her life had influenced her behavior and personality. Once she realized the source of her guilt feelings, she was able to find help and begin the recovery process.

HEALTHY VS. UNHEALTHY GUILT

Lest you feel that we think all guilt is bad, let us quickly note that guilt can be a very healthy thing. When a child steals something and feels guilty because he knows this is wrong, the guilt may motivate him to confess his deed and return the stolen item. This is positive. Similarly, if a married adult has had a promiscuous affair which he or she knows violates the marriage vows, he or she may feel so guilty they will end the affair and initiate a request for forgiveness from the offended spouse. Thus, all guilt is not bad. For a fact, a certain element of guilt gives perspective and balance to our moral sense of right and wrong.

Guilt goes awry, however, when it is false guilt: that is, when people feel guilty over phantom guilts that have been concocted by exaggerating circumstances or situations. For example, we have had people come for counseling who were told all their lives by an abusive mother, "You're going to be the death of me yet." When the mother finally died, the son or daughter somehow actually felt responsible for that death. This guilt became a lifelong burden. In reality, the mother was a nag, plain and simple, and she died of natural causes. There was no reason to feel guilty about this death (relieved, perhaps, but certainly not guilty).

People too often confuse guilt with shame. Guilt is how a person feels about something he or she did that was wrong. If a person backs out of the driveway and hits someone's car parked on the street and then drives away without reporting it, that individual will feel guilty about a wrongful act he or she has done. To atone, this person will need to go back, admit having caused the accident, and ask to pay for the damage repair.

Shame, however, is how a person feels about who he or she is as a person. The prayer of a person who's guilty is, "Lord, forgive me for what I've done." The prayer of a person with shame is, "Lord, forgive me for who I am." These are two entirely different things.

The reason guilt and shame are confused is because when a person does something that is wrong he feels guilty about the deed *and* embarrassed over the fact that his character could have been so weak ever to have committed such an act. To remedy the situation, he makes reparations for the wrongful deed; this satisfies the person who has been offended by him. The injured party "forgives" the guilty person. However, *the guilty person forgets to forgive himself!* And that's where the shame comes in.

Instead, the guilty person begins to speculate about his moral condition: "I must really be an evil person if I am capable of thinking and acting that way . . . It's a wonder I wasn't arrested and sent to jail for such behavior . . . I can't be much of a quality person if I would stoop to do something that terrible . . . If bad things start to happen to me in life, it will be because I deserve punishment . . . Everyone said I'd never amount to anything, and this foul deed I've done just proves how right they were."

When guilt advances to shame, it is often because a person has been victimized. That victimization has made that individual think he or she is evil and *is* the problem.

A normal person who has done something wrong would say, "That was a stupid thing for me to do. I just panicked and ran. The *situation* was upsetting and I responded inappropriately. I feel guilty about that and I'm going to take steps to amend what I've done."

A person ridden with shame would say, "*I, personally,* am a stupid thing. There's no hope for me. I do bad things because I am a bad person and, consequently, that's why bad things continue to happen to me. There's no way out of this, no way to make up for what I've done, no way to be anything other than the evil, low-life individual that I am."

SEPARATING GUILT AND SHAME

One of the reasons many people develop this kind of assessment of themselves is because in early years they felt their parents were ashamed of them. Such shame is sometimes a feeling a person has about himself that is based not on anything that was actually said aloud but implied in voice tone and body language by someone else. A dad might have said, "This is my son Tom, the baseball champ. Oh . . . yeah, and this is my other kid, Maurice. He ain't much for sports." Although the father never actually said that Maurice was useless in his eyes because he couldn't play baseball, Maurice sensed that this was the implication of what his father said. As such, Maurice will grow up feeling he is a second-rate person because his father had such a low opinion of him.

In dealing with children, it is crucial that the adult deal with guilt without creating shame. Let us show you the difference with a simple illustration. Imagine that Gaylen's daughter had accidentally left the gate open and the family dog got out.

To assign the guilt where it is due, yet not create an injunction of shame, Gaylen might say something like this. "Honey, this morning you forgot to close the gate and the dog got out. Fortunately, I found him and brought him back home. Now, we all make mistakes and we all forget things from time to time, but it's very dangerous for a little dog like this to run loose in the streets. I want you to promise me that you'll be much more careful from now on."

Now, Gaylen's daughter would see that her carelessness had put her pet in potential danger and had been an annoyance to her father. She would feel guilty about her actions. She would apologize to her dad, promise to be more careful from then on, and, for a fact, would be more careful. She had made an error and she had amended for it. The incident was concluded.

If, however, Gaylen had decided to give more weight to his admonition, he might have added an element of personal shame to his daughter's actions. The conversation would have sounded more like this. "You've never been able to remember a thing I tell you. All summer you've left that yard gate open. Today you nearly killed your dog. He got out and I barely was able to get him home before he was hit by a truck. I'm warning you, Miss Airhead, you'd better get your head out of the clouds and back down to earth. If this dog gets killed, you're not getting another pet. I told your mother you weren't responsible enough to have a pet to begin with. I don't know why we ever trusted you with a dog."

The message here is very different from the first message. Now, the daughter is being told she is stupid, not dependable, harmful to animals, disrespectful to her parents, and totally worthless. Not only is she guilty about not caring properly for her dog, she is ashamed of herself because her father doesn't respect her and doesn't trust her. She can start to lock the yard gate and solve that problem, but she cannot shake the feeling that she is a pathetic, irresponsible person who is unworthy of being loved by her parents and unworthy of owning a pet. Add to this a few more similar incidents and this young lady will grow up preprogrammed to equate every guilty feeling she has with an element of personal shame.

A PARDON FROM GUILT

Obviously, then, people can develop a sense of shame from what their parents (or teachers or siblings or friends) told them directly about themselves or what they implied about them in the *way* they talked to them. In either case, guilt and shame become synonymous and lifelong problems ensue. Fortunately, it usually is never too late to take steps to reverse this situation.

If feelings of guilt need to be dealt with in your life or in the life of someone you care about, we suggest you seek competent help.

SUMMARY

We've learned several important things about guilt in this chapter. We first learned that a sense of guilt is often confused with a feeling of shame, although the two are really very different. We next learned that unless guilt is dealt with, it can contribute to anxiety, depression, and poor self-image. It may even lead to suicide.

We further saw that false guilt is the guilt we allow others to impose on us for something we really should not have felt guilty about to begin with. These "guilt trips" are often enforced by aspects of shame, which are implied through statements of worthlessness imposed on us by other people.

Finally, we discovered that through recovery there are positive ways we can separate shame from guilt and then deal with whatever is actual guilt. We learned that no one has to go through life feeling guilty.

If you would like to do additional reading on the subject of coping with guilt, we have recommended several books at the end of this book.

17

Afraid of the Dark

When Fear Holds You Back

A farmer in Louisville was deathly afraid of flying. He wanted nothing to do with airplanes. Then one day the farmer's brother died and the burial was scheduled to be held in Seattle in two days. In order to get there on time, the farmer had to go by airplane.

Reluctantly, the farmer boarded the plane and made the trip. When he arrived in Seattle, his brother's family met him at the airport.

"Well," they asked, "how'd you like flying?"

"Hated it," responded the farmer. "I was afraid to put my full weight down on that seat the entire trip."

Like this farmer, many people go through life afraid of things there is no need to fear; and, also like the farmer, these people often try to cope with their fears in ways that are illogical, ineffective, and even irresponsible.

Years ago, President Roosevelt made a speech on radio in which he told Americans during World War II, "The only thing we have to fear is fear itself." One little boy listening at home said, "Well, I'm plenty 'feared' of fear already!"

Have you ever felt that way? Perhaps you know someone who seems to be abnormally afraid of even routine things in life? If you suspect that the fears you or someone you're concerned about are not normal, pause a moment to take the following test. Place a check mark in front of every statement that is true.

Does This Person Have a Problem with Fear?

☐ 1. This person avoids going outside of home because of fear.
☐ 2. This person is often haunted by fear when going to sleep at night.
☐ 3. This person has fears about traveling in an airplane or automobile or about riding in an elevator.
☐ 4. This person has turned down a promotion or transfer because of fear of new responsibilities or moving.
☐ 5. This person avoids developing friendships or new relationships because of distrust and fear.
☐ 6. This person avoids social gatherings, club or church activities, or holiday get-togethers because of fear.
☐ 7. This person has experienced a sense of suffocation when in certain closed-in environments, such as small rooms, crowded meeting rooms, elevators, train cars, taxis, or buses.
☐ 8. This person has experienced sudden anxiety attacks in public places such as a grocery store or library for no apparent reason.
☐ 9. This person has a haunting fear of impending death.
☐ 10. This person is terrified of certain bugs or animals.

As always, we caution you that this quiz is not meant to be a substitute for a complete psychological or emotional analysis by a licensed therapist or counselor. However, it may offer a perspective on the fear problems being faced by you or someone you are concerned about.

If you marked one or more statements, we urge you to give some serious thought to what that may mean in this person's life. Obviously, the more statements you marked, the more it means there is a possibility of a problem and the need for some kind of professional evaluation to know for sure.

CHILDHOOD TERRORS

When Walt Disney's color cartoon *The Three Little Pigs* was released, it featured a song entitled, "Who's Afraid of the

Big, Bad Wolf?" The implied answer was that the little pigs were the ones who were afraid. In reality, however, practically every child sitting in the theater watching the big, bad wolf—with his saliva dripping lips, huge fangs, and "huffed and puffed" up chest —was just as afraid as those pigs. Children scare easily, and sometimes they are ill equipped at ways of coping with their fears. Continuous fears and phobias have definite roots, however, such as dysfunctional families or abuse.

A humorous story is told of a little boy whose mother told him to go down into the basement to fetch her some clothespins. The child went to the top of the dark stairwell, took two steps down, then rushed back up to the kitchen.

"It's dark down there and I'm afraid," said the little boy.

"Now, now, don't be silly," responded the mother. "There's no need to be afraid. Haven't I always told you that the good Lord is forever with you? You're never alone. Now go down and get those clothespins for me."

Reluctantly, the little boy returned to the stairwell. Cautiously and hesitantly, he went four steps down into the darkness. Suddenly, he turned and ran back upstairs. He came back to his mother and announced, "Me and the Lord don't like it down there!"

Now, as comical as that story may be, the reality of the situation is that the little boy handled his dilemma quite well: if something is too scary to handle, avoid it. We only wish that all children would have a chance to escape their terrifying circumstances. Some don't, however, and that frequently leads to abnormal fears later in life.

A patient of Gaylen's, whom we'll call Trevor, was a perfect example of how childhood fears can later manifest trauma during adulthood.

Trevor was a well-to-do international business executive. He earned an excellent income as an art dealer and antique broker for a very elite clientele. His work frequently took him to Europe, the Middle East, Asia, and Mexico.

Trevor had been married for nine years to a lovely and charming woman. The couple had one child, a five-year-old son named Martin. The family lived in an attractive, modern home, and from all appearances seemed to be happy and content.

Then one month some bizarre things began to happen to Trevor. On a flight to Honolulu for a week of vacation with his wife, Trevor suddenly became claustrophobic. The walls of the plane seemed to close in on him. His heart began to pound rapidly, his face became flushed, he forehead was beaded with sweat. He found it hard to breathe. The flight attendant put an oxygen mask on Trevor and placed a cold compress against the base of his neck. In time, he recovered, but he still felt weakened by the whole ordeal.

Three days later, while in Honolulu, Trevor got into the elevator to go up to his hotel room on the fourteenth floor. When the doors closed, the feeling of claustrophobia again overwhelmed him. His knees buckled, his hands began to shake, the collar button on his shirt seemed to be choking him. When the elevator finally stopped and the doors opened, Trevor fell into the hallway outside.

A visit to an emergency room revealed no physical disorders. Trevor's heart was healthy, his lungs were clear, and his muscle tone was excellent. Upon returning to California, he made an appointment to see Gaylen to talk about what happened.

Gaylen asked him if there had been any recent changes in his life—a new job, a move to a new home, the death of a parent—anything that might have triggered these panic attacks. Trevor said there had been no changes. Then Gaylen asked Trevor how old his son was.

"He's five," answered Trevor. "In fact, he just turned five a couple of weeks ago. We had a big party for him with a cake and presents and lots of neighborhood kids over for games."

Gaylen began to suspect what might be going on. He asked, "Trevor, have you ever thought about the ways that you and your son are alike?"

Trevor thought for a moment, then said, "Yeah. My son and I are amazingly alike. I see a lot of myself in him."

This led to a more detailed discussion of Trevor's own childhood. He seemed willing to talk about his early years, but he did it with some difficulty, as though it had been some time since he had thought about it.

Gaylen decided to give him some homework assignments to help Trevor fill in some of what were apparently obscured or missing memories from his own childhood. For example, Gaylen asked Trevor to go home and look through any family photo albums or any other documents or keepsakes from pre-school or elementary school years. He also asked him to make note of any of the feelings that he had when walking through some of those memories. He told him to keep a diary of any dreams that he might have during the next several weeks.

Gaylen knew that these kinds of anxiety attacks were frequently the result of emotionally injurious experiences on the part of a person who had not been able to deal with them at the time they occurred.

Sure enough, within a short period of time Trevor began to recall the sickening sensations of having been hauled into a hall closet in his home by an adult neighbor and sexually molested.

That was when he was five years old.

When his son reached the same age as when Trevor's own trauma had occurred, it stirred the buried feelings about the most frightening event of his life, and that erupted in the form of the panic attacks that he experienced on his business trip. Being in an enclosed space like the airplane or the elevator suddenly became so similar to the smothering experience of being in the hall closet, he could barely stand it.

Trevor should have been able to tell someone he trusted what had happened to him at the time that it occurred, and he should have been able to receive the kind of comfort and assurance that he needed. That would have started his recovery immediately. Like many victims of molestation, however, the experience was so traumatic and the neighbor had so overpowered him and threatened him as a protective measure, Trevor unconsciously buried the facts of what happened and continued with his life without having to think about it. Now, at the age of thirty-nine, he was beginning the process of healing for the first time, and with Gaylen's help he experienced tremendous emotional healing at a deep level and the panic attacks gradually disappeared.

FEARS AND DISORDERS

Many people do not realize that specific fears they may have are actually conditions that have names, identifiable behavior patterns, and common consequences. For example, arachnophobia is the fear of spiders; agoraphobia is the fear of people or crowds; claustrophobia is the fear of confined spaces. Some people even have phobphobia—the fear of being afraid.

Childhood wariness of darkened rooms or loud barking dogs or strange surroundings is very normal. It's an instinctive system of self-preservation. It takes time to adjust to situations or things one has never experienced before.

Usually, people learn to adapt more readily as they grow older. The first time a loud burst of thunder is heard, it may be terrifying. Subsequent thunderstorms, however, are far less fearsome. The first day of kindergarten may be frightening for a child, but the first day of third grade is no big deal. People mature. They gain perspective on things. They realize that what they originally perceived as having potential danger is really nothing to be afraid of.

For a person who has experienced deep emotional injury or trauma in childhood, however, the childlike part of that person takes refuge in an emotional closet in order to try to deal with the pain; it becomes trapped there. Also trapped are childlike understandings of things like fear, and they can remain there even while the rest of the person grows into adulthood. It isn't until the person has the opportunity to safely walk back to that closet and open it and feel the feelings that are in there and process those pains that recovery begins to take place.

Rich counseled a man in his mid-thirties who went to bed at night afraid to turn off the light because he worried that someone might sneak into his room through the bedroom window and "get" him.

This man had had the same fear as a child, but he hadn't

told anyone about it. Later, as a married adult, these nightly fear fixations led to great problems in his marriage. He sought counseling. He was surprised to learn that his fear was not normal. It turned out to be related to having been raised in an alcoholic home where there was physical and emotional abuse and nighttime arguments between his parents.

For many people, such as this man who feared the dark, the road to recovery begins with basic knowledge. These people are taught three things right away: (1) there is a name for what you have been experiencing; (2) other people have had this same problem; and (3) hope exists to discover the reason why you have this disorder and, thereby, also to discover a way to recover from it. Once a person can say, "I understand more about myself and about what is at the root of my disorder," that individual immediately has more control over the events in his or her life. And, in time, control leads to stability.

NORMAL FEAR

We should caution you that not all experiences of anxiety or fear, even as adults, are indications of abnormal problems. Physical changes, such as PMS, hormonal adjustments, or menopause, make some people more susceptible to feelings of anxiety and apprehension. Similarly, a new episode in life can seem scarier than it is: brides or grooms sometimes faint during marriage ceremonies; many people get "the shakes" when it comes time to sign that first home mortgage; elderly people have been known to take several weeks to adjust to new surroundings in a retirement home because they are afraid of the many strangers around them. Additionally, stress can create new levels of anxiety: if one goes without adequate sleep for five days, an innate sense of "survival fear" can develop.

These temporary bouts with fear are usually cured with the passing of time. Once you've made a couple of mortgage payments, home ownership becomes enjoyable. Once you've settled into the retirement community, the scary strangers become new friends. These are evidences of maturity. A child stays afraid because he has no skills for coping with whatever is scaring him. An adult works through frightening events by adapting, working, correcting, adjusting, and protecting.

If you feel that you or someone you are concerned about needs help to to overcome a certain fear, let us make a few suggestions you can follow:

A. *Keep a journal.* Carefully note the time, place, and events related to the start of an anxiety attack or sudden sense of fear. How frequently do these episodes occur? At what time of day or night? At what locations? What other people were present? What sort of business or pleasure activity were you involved in? This information may show you a behavioral pattern that will reveal the basis for your fear. Begin to look for a common thread between them. If you seek counseling, show your journal to your therapist.

B. *Join a support group.* People who share common disorders find it comforting to share their experiences with other people who really understand the problems and can relate to them. For information on support groups, contact your local hospitals or write to the National Mental Health Association, 1021 Prince Street, Alexandria, Virginia 22314–2971.

C. *Arrange to be given a physical examination.* Your family physician will be able to determine if there are hormonal changes occurring in your body or elements of sickness you might not be aware of. Treating these problems may alleviate other problems related to fear or anxiety.

D. *Seek professional counseling.* The guidance of a therapist in helping you deal with your fears can greatly assist your recovery. You family physician or pastor can make a referral for you or you can call Alpha Counseling at 1–800-23-ALPHA.

E. *Do additional reading about fears.* Your local public library or area bookstores will have books that will give you more background on fears, anxiety, and disorders.

SUMMARY

We have seen in this chapter that fear provides a natural defense mechanism for us when we are children. If something looks scary, we try to avoid it. Many adults who have deeply rooted fears must identify the source of these fears, process the pain associated with these fears, and then find counseling in order to recover.

18

Everything Seems Gray

When Depression Is a Companion

When actress Patty Duke-Astin wrote her autobiography, *Call Me Anna* (Toronto: Bantam Books, 1987), and admitted she was a manic depressive, it amazed the public for two reasons: first, because no one could believe that a woman who had recorded four hit record albums, had earned an Academy Award, had had her own television show, and had been elected President of the Screen Actors Guild *could actually be* the victim of "mental problems"; and second, because, even if she was having mental and emotional problems, *surely* she wouldn't want the public to know about it!

This, however, was the precise reason why Patty wanted to reveal her long-hidden secret. She knew that literally thousands of people suffer from various forms of depression, but an estimated 75 percent of them never seek help because there is a stigma of being labeled "a basket case" or "a nut" or "a psycho."

Patty knew she wasn't insane (although she feared this before being properly diagnosed). She believed that if the public could hear her story, people might be less resistant to seeking counseling for ongoing bouts of depression.

Recent history shows how poorly informed the public actually is about depression and how this lack of information can create unfounded fears. When Sen. Thomas F. Eagleton ran for Vice President on the Democratic ticket in 1972 with Sen. George McGovern, it was learned that Sen. Eagleton had visited a counselor's office a few times to discuss some problems he was having with "blue moods" and lethargy.

When the newspapers reported this, it sounded as though the senator had been undergoing intensive psychiatric treatment. The result was that Sen. Eagleton felt he had to resign his candidacy. R. Sargent Shriver replaced him. The Democrats, overshadowed by the Eagleton episode, lost by a landslide (47 million votes went to Richard Nixon and more than a million votes went to John Anderson, an independent candidate).

It is our hope that readers of our book will come to know that professional counseling is as valid a help to people as any of the many areas of physical medicine. There should be no stigma attached to psychological treatment.

Having said that, we nevertheless realize that old images are hard to dispel. In fact, one of the chief motivations we have had for writing this book has been to provide some insights into emotional disorders for people who would never otherwise set up an appointment with a therapist. If you are in that category, we hope you will gain a new perspective on the validity of counseling by the time you have completed this book. In the meantime, the following list of statements will help you determine whether you or someone you are concerned about may have a problem with depression. Put a check mark in the space before any statement that is true.

Is This Person's Depression a Problem?

☐ 1. This person's personal grooming and hygiene have deteriorated.
☐ 2. This person's sex drive has decreased.

☐ 3. This person's appetite for food has decreased noticeably.
☐ 4. This person feels a sense of hopelessness.
☐ 5. This person no longer enjoys parties, club meetings, or church attendance.
☐ 6. This person seems to be losing the will to live or talks increasingly about death.
☐ 7. This person feels overwhelmed by even the smallest details of life.
☐ 8. This person's has begun to isolate himself or herself from other people.
☐ 9. This person has trouble getting normal sleep because of worry or emotional pain.
☐ 10. This person increasingly is having a hard time concentrating.

As always, we caution you that this quiz is not meant to be a substitute for a complete psychological and emotional analysis by a licensed practioner. It may, however, give you some perspective on feelings of depression you or someone you know is experiencing.

If you marked at least two of these statements, we urge you to put some serious thought into what it means about this person's life. Obviously, the more statements you marked, the more it means there is the possibility of a problem and the need for some kind of professional evaluation to know for sure.

THE RANGE OF DEPRESSION

Approximately one in every twenty Americans is suffering from some form of depression. Two out of three people dealing with depression are female. Researchers believe there are several reasons for the higher number of women: (1) men are resolution oriented, which makes them seek an end to a problem even if it requires blunt behavior, whereas women are more enduring and long-suffering and, thus, easier targets for a buildup of unresolved, depressing elements; (2) men have been conditioned to bear their burdens privately, whereas women will more readily talk about themselves and their problems to other people; although talking about problems is

extremely beneficial when it is done with a licensed therapist, it can be very detrimental when it is done with friends
who only concur that, yes, you *do* have a miserable life and,
indeed, there does seem to be *no hope* for your situation; (3)
whereas men are expected to take risks in business and develop an entrepreneurial spirit, most women prefer a bedrock
base of stability and security; as such, too much instability
and insecurity can cause worry, anxiety, and depression in
women; and (4) depression is often correlated with emotional
injury, and more women than men have been reported to
have been abused.

But whether in men or women, depression is debilitating.
Fifteen out of one hundred people suffering from extreme
depression will commit suicide, and ten others will try but
fail. This includes children, teenagers, and adults of all ages.
Depression can be correlated with insomnia, headaches,
paranoia, loss of appetite, a sense of dread and fear, anger,
loss of concentration, inability to sustain religious faith, and
strong feelings of loneliness and alienation.

It's quite normal to have a "down day" or even "an off
week." If your best friend moves away, it takes a while to adjust. If your pet cat dies, you can't forget it in a day. If it's
Christmas and your son or daughter is doing military service
overseas, you'll feel the absence. If the proposal you worked
hard on gets rejected by your client, you're bound to feel both
exhausted and angry for a couple of days.

Life has some tough times for all of us, and it's silly to put
on a Pollyanna smile and say, "Hey, no problem" when inter-
nally we feel like someone has just kicked us in the stomach.
Life does knock us down sometimes. Eventually, however, if
we are emotionally healthy, we will see that the sun is still
coming up each day, the earth is still turning, and life (believe
it or not) is still going on. So, we rejoin the living and get back
into the race. As Robert Anthony Schuller said in his book
Getting Through the Going-Through Stage (New York: Ballantine, 1988), "It's not a sin to lose, but it is a tragedy to give
up."

Most people agree with this. They may experience a temporary bout with depression, but when they stop to think about all the good there still is in their lives, they pull themselves up by the bootstraps and go forward.

But what about the people who don't seem to be able to do this? For them, one bout of depression is linked to another, then another, and then yet another, until the emotional and psychological burdens manifest themselves in physical and behavioral malfunctions.

For Patty Duke-Astin, a manic depressive, there were periods in her life of exuberance and dynamism in which she could sing, act, conduct business matters, and care for her family. Alternately, however, were periods when she lost control of herself and she would break furniture, smash dishes, not report to work, or get involved in sexual affairs with men for whom she had no affection. After many years of such radical behavior swings, she regained control of her life through a combination of prescribed medications and professional counseling.

Research has shown that some depression is physical, whereas other depression is emotional or psychological. There is a very strong correlation between depression and early childhood emotional injury in our observation. Since depression can be the root problem of so many of the disorders we discussed in Section One of this book, it must never be taken lightly. Depressed people need help.

SUMMARY

In this chapter we discovered that temporary depression is something all people experience from time to time. It's normal. One must expect a certain number of depressing events in life. The important thing is to put the situation behind us and move on.

We learned that some people, however, may have a physical disorder that causes depression. Often, medications are needed for depression. Counseling can often help people who have experienced emotional traumas to gain skills for recognizing and coping with depression and the roots of depression.

For additional studies related to the causes of depression and ways of dealing with it, we have provided a reading list at the back of the book.

PART THREE:

Where Did All This Pain Come From?

The Importance of Recognizing Emotional Injury

I Always Thought It Was My Fault

The Devastation of Sexual Abuse

Although sexual harassment gained a lot of press coverage during the nomination hearings of Supreme Court Justice Clarence Thomas, sexual abuse has too long remained the "silent" problem.

People have their own stereotype as to what molestation consists of, but many people think that unless there has been sexual intercourse there hasn't been molestation or incest. The truth is, all sexual abuse includes more than intercourse, and all sexual abuse is harmful, whether it involves intercourse or not.

Nobody knows exactly how many people in our country are victims of sexual abuse, but everyone who deals with it agrees that the statistics are just a shadow of what's really going on. Most incidents of sexual abuse never get reported, and the number of adults who are dealing with sexual molestation issues is at almost epidemic proportions.

Many people don't realize that they are victims of sexual abuse because they have never viewed what happened to them as molestation or they repressed what happened to them (see chapter 22 for more information about this). The ordeal was so traumatic, they blocked it from their memory.

If you or someone you are concerned about may feel there is a problem with sexual abuse, pause now to read the following list of statements. Put a check mark in front of each one you feel applies to the person you have in mind.

Is Sexual Molestation, Incest, or Abuse a Problem?

❑ 1. In childhood there was some kind of sexual contact with an adult.

❑ 2. In childhood there was an experience of being overpowered sexually by another person.

❑ 3. There seem to be sexual extremes in this person's life such as an addiction to sex or a lack of interest in sex or a lack of sexual desire.

❑ 4. This person has had a history of being terrified of darkness or of feeling trapped.

❑ 5. This person has had recurring nightmares either as a child or as an adult.

❑ 6. This person has bouts of fear or panic for no explainable reason.

❑ 7. This person is plagued by recurring depression.

❑ 8. This person has a problem with anger or rage.

❑ 9. Guilt and shame seem to be themes in this person's life.

❑ 10. This person has difficulty trusting other people or God.

❑ 11. This person has an eating disorder.

❑ 12. This person seems out of touch with personal feelings.

❑ 13. This person has trouble with intimacy.

❑ 14. This person is uncomfortable with sex or sexuality.

❑ 15. This person seems to have a negative attitude about his or her body or feels disconnected from the body.

❑ 16. This person has felt overpowered by another person verbally through unwanted conversation about sex.

❑ 17. This person has had his or her sexual space invaded by another person through being coerced or forced to disrobe unwillingly or by being spied upon while in the bedroom or bathroom.

❑ 18. This person seems deeply troubled or even traumatized by stories about rape or molestation.

❑ 19. There are important people from this person's childhood whom this person seems to hate.

❑ 20. This person has a preoccupation with his or her body or with bodily appearance.

If you marked any of these statements, we urge you to give some serious thought as to what that means to this person's life. Obviously, the more statements you marked, the more it means there is a possibility of a problem and the need for some kind of professional evaluation to know for sure.

THE HIDDEN ABUSE

One of the characteristics of someone who has been sexually abused is that the person typically has either never talked about it with anyone else or, if that person has discussed the incident, the reaction was such that he or she decided never to talk about it again. As such, vast numbers of people have gone into adulthood carrying the debris from one of the most devastating things that has ever happened to them. They haven't shared this with anyone, so they have had no way to process the pain toward healing. As a result, it comes out in different ways in their life as long as it is unprocessed.

Take the case of a woman of thirty-five who has a daughter eight years old. When the mother was eight, she was sexually abused. However, the event was so traumatic, she internalized it and pretended it didn't happen. When her daughter turned eight, all of a sudden the mother fell apart emotionally. It was as though someone had pushed a button and suddenly all of the unprocessed trauma that had been in her came to the surface. Her body tried to process those feelings, but she didn't have the tools to process them when she was much younger.

A person who has been abused very frequently becomes frozen at the age that he or she shut down. Many adults who seem painfully childlike (not in a delightful way but rather in an immature way) are emotionally still at that age because they have not grown through their painful experience. Often, we grow through painful experiences that help us mature. A victim, however, has taken refuge in a bomb shelter at the age of the traumatic incident, and he or she shuts down because of all the pain.

Almost every promiscuous person we have counseled has been a victim of molestation. Incest, particularly, is destructive and devastating.

Rich Buhler counseled a man who said he was heartbroken because his daughter had accused him of not responding to the needs in her life. The man said, "I have four children and the other three grew up quite normal. I honestly believe that my wife and I paid equal attention to all of our children. I just don't understand why my daughter feels neglected."

Rich asked the man if it was possible his daughter had ever been sexually abused. He said he knew of no such incident. As time went by, however, the daughter became so depressed she had to be placed in a hospital to prevent her from attempting suicide. While there and in counseling, the girl came in touch with her memories and discovered that she had been sexually molested by a school worker more than once when she was in elementary school.

This incident bears out the fact that there are some children who are now adults and who would describe themselves as being victims of neglect on the part of their parents but who were, in fact, victims of molestation outside their home. They resent the fact that Mom and Dad did not give them the kind of emotional nourishment that they wanted. In reality, the parents had nothing to do with this problem. This person was emotionally shut down by an experience with sexual abuse.

THE FRIEND WHO MOLESTS

Most people who are sexually abused have been abused by someone they know or trust, such as a relative or family friend. The stereotype that many people have of a molester is someone who roams the neighborhood in a van and lures children into his van with candy, then abducts and rapes them. Sadly, that does happen, and that's why we need to teach children to say no to strangers. However, most molesters fit a different description.

The vast majority of children who are abused in any way—whether physically, sexually, or emotionally—suffer at the hands of someone they know and have reason to trust (parents, relatives, the school playground supervisor, a church nursery volunteer). Many people who have been sexually abused don't regard themselves as victims because they believe a molester is a stranger who abducts people off the street. If the molestation happened with Uncle Harry while the family was at the mountain cabin, it doesn't seem like molestation. Patients will say, "It's just that Uncle Harry was a little weird."

Rich dealt with a man who very obviously had deep issues of emotional injuries and starvation and who was having terrible troubles in his marriage. The couple wanted to save and improve the quality of their marriage. The wife was in counseling, but the husband wasn't helping her improve the marriage.

The man came to see Rich, and the troubles he described himself having caused Rich to ask if the man had experienced any form of sexual abuse as a youngster. The man said no, but as Rich used a series of specific questions to probe the root of the man's problem, it turned out that the man had been deeply involved in a whole range of sexual activities throughout his entire childhood. He had had sexual encounters with an adult recreational director, as well as numerous children in the recreation group. Because so many children were involved and because it went on for so many years, the man actually thought this was not molestation. When Rich explained to the man that he had experienced molestation, the man began to understand why he was having problems as an adult.

It should be noted that it is normal for children to be sexually curious about each other. Just because two youngsters play doctor or show interest in each other's bodies, that does not mean abuse is going on. Nevertheless, even children of the same age can be on different sexual development levels, and it is possible for one to overpower the other sexually. If a child has been abused sexually, he or she often develops a drive to do the same thing to other children. The molested child will try to duplicate what has been done to him or her.

It is important for people who have been sexually abused to seek counseling. Their own interpretation of the events of what happened to them will range from self-accusation ("It was my fault this happened") to denial ("That never happened to me") and from misunderstanding ("This is what all children do") to misdirected blame ("My parents didn't pay enough attention to me"). It takes an experienced counselor to help the victim of sexual abuse get to the root of the problem and begin to deal with it.

20

My Folks Were a Little Strict, That's All

Identifying Physical Abuse

It is shocking when someone finally recognizes that the mistreatment he or she has been enduring for a long time from a family member or friend or employer might be considered abuse.

It is crushing when someone finally recognizes that the treatment he or she has been handing out to people around them is abuse.

When thinking of abuse, it's easy to have a picture in our minds of an unshaven, drunken bruiser of a man who yells obscenities at a frightened child. That, of course, is a scene of abuse, and far too many people have experienced it, but the fact is, people who act abusively toward those around them come in every category and description. They are both the young and the old, the good-looking and not, the educated and uneducated, those who are social and those who are unsociable, and those who are religious and those who are not. They can be male or female, parents or children, husbands or wives, relatives or friends, employers or co-workers.

Some forms of abuse are physical, such as hitting or shoving or pinching or squeezing or kicking or any other way of causing hurt to the body. Other forms of abuse are emotional. They may not involve hurting the body, but they have just as devastating an effect on the person experiencing them. The abuser may use verbal insults or cursing, mental ambushes or degradation. Cruel treatments may be used, such as locking someone in a closet or taking prized possessions away from a child (or having them broken or thrown away by a parent).

One of the most memorable phone calls Rich Buhler ever received on his radio program was from a woman who was emotionally devastated one Christmas morning when her cruel parents, in an act of anger, gave her a wrapped box of fireplace ashes as her only present. It was meant to humiliate and shame her, and it did—*for life!*

Some abuse, of course, crosses the line into the legal arena, and a person can be arrested for it. There is abusive behavior, however, that is not illegal even though it can be just as damaging. It is important for people to recognize this and to take some courageous steps to do something about it. Read the following list of statements and assess whether or not you see yourself or somebody you know:

Is There a Situation of Abuse?

☐ 1. People have told this person his or her behavior is abusive.
☐ 2. This person has had body contact with another person, such as pushing, squeezing, or hitting.
☐ 3. This person punishes others who have tried to say anything negative or critical to him or her.
☐ 4. This person insists on controlling another person's schedule, activities, and contact with other people, demanding permission for almost anything.
☐ 5. This person has been arrested or threatened with arrest for mistreatment of someone else.
☐ 6. This person goes into rages in front of others and throws things or curses or insults others when angry.
☐ 7. This person has an attitude of punishing those around him or her for having needs and expressing them.
☐ 8. This person verbally or physically overpowers other people sexually.

☐ 9. This person uses anger and rage as tools of manipulation.
☐ 10. This person has experienced physical, emotional, or sexual abuse and has found himself or herself treating other people in some of the same ways.

While the above test is not meant to be a substitute for a complete analysis by a competent therapist, it will help you determine whether or not such an analysis might be beneficial. If you marked any of the above statements, we urge you to put some serious thought into what it means about this person's life. Obviously, the more statements you marked, the more it means there is the possibility of a problem and the need for some kind of professional evaluation to know for sure.

WHAT DO I DO IF I'M BEING ABUSED?

How you respond to abuse depends on the severity of the abuse that you are experiencing. Response options range from simply trying to improve the relationship with the abuser to actually taking legal action.

The first step is to let yourself gradually admit that what is going on may actually be abuse. That will help you make more definitive decisions about what to do. The second step is to get help. Start by doing some reading about abusive or controlling relationships. Also, start talking to people who have experienced such relationships and who have had to make some tough decisions about them.

If by legal definition (and you can check with your local authorities on this) you are being abused by another person, our recommendation is to seek safety as quickly as possible and to ensure the safety of anyone else who may be in danger, such as children. Even if you love the person who is abusing you and you want to try to continue having a relationship with that person, you do not need to tolerate abuse or have to live in fear and danger. If it is your goal to improve the relationship with the abuser, then the abuse must be effectively confronted and any decisions you make about the future need to be influenced by whether or not the abuser is really going to take the problem seriously.

If you truly fear for your life, there are hotlines available in most cities for persons who are being abused. There are agencies and facilities that specialize in offering you a place to stay that will be completely safe and unknown to whoever is a threat to you.

We recommend that you read some literature about abuse and abusers and that you find a support group or a counselor in your area who has special knowledge and understanding of abusive relationships. If you are literally being prohibited from talking with anyone or going anywhere, try to give the abuse hotline a call and tell your story and ask for confidential help.

You can also be aided greatly if you know someone who has survived an abusive relationship and who can give you support and advice. In our experience many people who have been treating others abusively have not realized that they have been abusive. There usually is intense denial because there is often love for the people they are abusing. Some of the abuse is even thought of in the mind of the abuser as being the result of love.

Rich Buhler had a friend in high school, a girl we'll call Rebeccah, whose father was an extremely abusive man. Although the father was a minister, he felt that his domineering, cruel way of ruling his family was for their own good.

Rebeccah seldom had adequate clothing and she was sensitive to the fact that she had to wear virtually the same clothes to school every day. It wasn't a matter of money. The family had enough support to provide for everybody's needs. The father, however, had an attitude that clothes were a necessary evil and the fewer, the better. Rebeccah bravely tried to adopt her father's values about clothes, but the pain of not having that most basic need met was deep and abiding. Rebeccah was also under intense pressure to perform academically and was physically punished if her grades were not up to par.

One of the worst moments Rich ever experienced was one

evening when Rebeccah's father decided to sponsor a talent show at his church and forced Rebeccah to be in it. She was supposed to sing, but she was frightened about it. She told her father that she didn't want to do it, but he regarded that as weakness on her part and ordered her to sing. When the time came for Rebeccah's song, she stood at the edge of the platform frozen with stage fright.

Concealing his anger, Rebeccah's father introduced the next performer. He then grabbed his daughter's arm and pulled her into the hallway, where he verbally pummeled her with shame.

Rich lost contact with Rebeccah after high school, but 20 years later he learned that Rebeccah had spent most of her adult life living in depression.

WHAT IF I AM THE ABUSER?

Most abusers view themselves as having a certain amount of caring for the people around them. Some even regard themselves as God's gift to mankind and are resistant to any suggestion that their conduct may be unhealthy. Because of this denial, it's a big challenge to get a person like that to admit that there's a problem, and for the person who has finally come through a season of acknowledging being abusive and seeing the impact it has had on other people, it's very painful. It's also a very courageous thing to do, however, and we have enormous admiration for those who are doing it.

John is a good example. He has been married for twenty-one years and is the father of three girls and one boy. John was reared in a home where there was genuine love but where physical abuse was the norm. John and his brothers and sisters had frequently been slapped, spanked, and hit and sometimes punished severely because the parents truly believed that was the best way to handle failure and misbehavior. John's father had been reared that way, and he was just doing what he had been taught was right.

The impact of this treatment on John and his siblings was injurious. John, however, entered adulthood with no clue that the behavior of his father and mother had been abusive.

He loved them and they loved him and he was sure of that. There were a lot of other wonderful things about his parents and his home that gave him many good memories.

When John got married and started having children, he handled discipline and punishment the same way his parents had. John's wife Elaine, however, was increasingly alarmed at his treatment of the children, and she tried to sound the warning alarm. She felt that John gave the children too many spankings and that they were too hard and were given for the wrong reasons. One day Elaine walked in on John when, in anger, he had pinned his oldest daughter to the wall while lecturing her about something he felt she had done wrong. The daughter was absolutely terrified.

When Elaine tried to talk with John about her concerns, he got angry and accused her of not being supportive of him as a father. He loved his kids. He was confident of that. How *dare* Elaine question that!

Years and many confrontations between Elaine and John went by, and as he got older and learned a little more about life, he started privately questioning whether or not there was a tiny bit of truth in what Elaine was saying. He felt bad about some events of anger with his children, and on occasion he had even gone back to a child he had mistreated and apologized. He still didn't think of it as abuse.

It was a crisis that finally brought things to a head. John's seven-year-old daughter, Ashley, had been deeply wounded by John's treatment of her, and she became the kind of person who would withdraw in fear when he started into a rage. One Saturday morning when John was trying to motivate the children to help with some clean-up chores around the house, he started to focus on Ashley.

Basically, Ashley had not done what John had assigned her to do, or at least she was being very slow about it. John began berating her and shaming her for not doing her assigned chore. The more she retreated emotionally, the angrier he got. He grabbed her violently by the arm, took her into a nearby bedroom, and gave her what amounted to a beating.

Two days later in school, the teacher spotted serious bruises where John had grabbed Ashley by the arm. The teacher had not suspected that anything bad had happened to Ashley, but she asked the little girl how she got the bruises. Ashley's reaction, however, caught the teacher's attention, for Ashley immediately showed a frightened look and retreated emotionally. It was obvious she had no intention of saying anything about the bruises.

Skillfully, the teacher was able to get Ashley to reveal enough about what had happened to warrant mentioning it to the school authorities. They, in turn, contacted a county agency in charge of protecting children. A subsequent investigation showed that Ashley's bruises from the spanking were severe enough to justify legal action.

Ashley was taken to a foster home for the night, and the county agents went to Ashley's home and took one of her sisters and her brother to foster homes too. The youngest child, an infant, was allowed to remain with Mom.

John suddenly found himself charged with suspected child abuse. He was furious. He was mad at the teacher for reporting what she saw and suspected. He was mad as well at the school for contacting the authorities. He was especially mad at the county agency for taking his children away from him. He became angry at anyone who would suggest that he had anything but the best interests in mind for his family.

After extensive evaluation by the case worker from the county, John and his family were brought back together within a few days, with the requirement that John seek counseling and that the family work together to become emotionally healthier.

"I was required to see a psychologist," John says, "and to attend a meeting with other men who had been involved in abusive behavior. At first, I was stubborn and resistant to the notion that I needed any help, but as time went by I began to realize how wrong I was. I was especially affected by hearing some of the other men's stories about their own victimization when they were children and, between that and the counseling, I began to see for the first time how broken I was from the treatment of my own father. We also went through family counseling and I heard from my own children's lips how hurt and frightened they were of me. That broke my heart."

John progressed beautifully. Because he really did love his family, he came to realize how much his behavior had hurt everyone and had been counterproductive to the very goals he had for his children. He courageously confronted his own pain and went through recovery for it. He fully acknowledged the pain his wife and children had endured and even went on to become an occasional speaker before church and men's groups, telling about what he had learned.

SUMMARY

If you have come to realize that you may be involved in behavior that is abusive to those around you, whether it be family or friends or employees, there are several steps you can take.

First, admit that there is a problem even if that admission is to yourself or to God only. Call it what it is. It's painful, but it's the beginning of an important new season in your life.

Second, reach out for help. You won't get through this by yourself. Support groups that are safe and confidential can be found through your local mental health agencies or law enforcement groups or perhaps a local church. There are also resources at the end of chapter 24 in this book that will be helpful to you.

Third, get counseling. Find a counselor who specializes in helping victims of abuse or those who have abused others.

Fourth, have hope. Even though there is a great deal of resentment and anger in our culture about those who have perpetrated abuse, there are also examples of healing and restoration. Through bravely confronting the issues and admitting the truth and getting help, you can be reconciled with those whom you have hurt and there can be a future. Both of us are convinced of that.

21

The Devil Did It to Me

The Problem of Satanic Ritual Abuse

Let us begin here by saying that we debated whether or not we should include a chapter on satanic ritual abuse in this book. It is a very controversial issue today among psychologists, law enforcement agencies, and religious leaders. Dealing with it in any manner is akin to working with dynamite—you had better know what you are doing.

Satanic ritual abuse is victimization that has occurred at the hands of an occultic or other kind of religious group and has resulted in deep destruction in the life of the person who experienced it. It typically involves sexual abuse but can include other kinds of injury as well, such as physical and emotional abuse.

Satanic Ritual Abuse (SRA) victims say they have been terrorized by their experiences and have flashbacks of memories of satanic symbols, satanic rituals, blood, bodies, murder, and even human sacrifice. SRA victims are frequently diagnosed as having multiple personality disorders or the apparent existence of several different "persons" living in the same body. This is because under extreme abuse, the victim can psychologically "split" into several different parts as a way of dealing with that which has been overwhelming.

There is great controversy as to whether Satanic Ritual Abuse really exists and, if so, how widespread it is. We have looked into the question carefully and have come to a couple of important conclusions.

First, we believe that SRA victims need to be treated with respect and compassion. Even though there may be some question as to what explains their victimization, we believe that each of them has been victimized and each needs to be treated as a deeply wounded person. Some critics of SRA believe that the victims have had the thoughts or memories of ritual abuse "planted" in their minds by their counselors or that they have become caught up in a kind of hysteria in response to the increased visibility of ritual abuse. We concur that there are some unwise and inexperienced counselors who may get preoccupied with a diagnosis like SRA, but the majority of counselors are handling their clients with as much professional balance as possible, and we believe the numbers of counselees, if any, who have had SRA memories induced upon them is small. We believe the victims. We believe they have experienced every bit of the terrifying ordeals they say they have. We don't believe they are lying or concocting what they are reporting.

On the other hand, it's been virtually impossible for SRA victims to substantiate what they've experienced with external, collaborating evidence. SRA supporters say that is because the abused happened under such secretive and protected circumstances, there would be no way to prove what happened apart from the memories of the person who experienced it. Critics of the SRA diagnosis say the reason it can't be proved is because it never actually happened.

Much more research and investigation will have to be done before we can settle the controversy, but we have no doubt that many SRA victims have been treated in exactly the way that they remember and that they have been severely emotionally injured as a result. They need to be helped into recovery.

We have elected not to do a self-test on ritual abuse because, except for the memories of ritualistic or satanic or occultic experiences, the symptoms are similar to other kinds of abuse, particularly sexual abuse. We also want to be cautious not to suggest to people who have been victimized in other ways that they may have experienced SRA. All abuse feels very dark and satanic.

There are many, however, who have little question about the existence of SRA and who diagnose and treat it. One of those is Mary Battles, a professional counselor from California who has spent many years working almost exclusively with SRA victims. Her experiences are good examples of those who believe in Satanic Ritual Abuse.

THE HIDDEN HORROR

Mary Battles completed a B.A. at San Diego State University and earned her master's degree in psychology from National University. She began her career as a therapist in San Diego County as a counselor at two retreat ranches created as recovery havens for delinquent or emotionally disturbed boys. Mary directed therapy sessions with parents and their sons.

In 1988 Mary joined the staff of Alpha Counseling, headed by Dr. Gaylen Larson. Mary initially worked with patients suffering from sexual abuse. On the occasions when it turned out that one of Mary's patients was a victim of ritual abuse, it seemed that Mary had an ability to help this person through the recovery. Soon, other counselors and doctors were referring their patients suffering from ritual abuse to Mary and, in time, this developed into an area of specialization for her. Between 1988 and 1992, Mary treated more than seventy-five people suffering from ritual abuse.

"The term 'ritual' is not used lightly in referring to what these people have undergone," explains Mary Battles. "The abuse they have encountered has been procedural, systematic, calculated, and heartless."

She adds, "It begins with a period of submissiveness indoctrination. The victim is whipped, starved, and tortured to the point that he or she will readily cooperate with any sort of cultic practice just to avoid further torture. Once this physical mastery has been obtained, the cult leaders then proceed to gain spiritual control. They direct the victims in ceremonies designed to invite demon possession of their souls. After this, the final step is to use the victim as an offering to the cultic gods. Sometimes the victim serves as a sex object in worship practices and is abused by everyone else in the cult. Other times he or she is murdered as a blood sacrifice."

Mary's findings show that ritual abuse frequently begins with incest. One of her patients, whom we'll call Dana, was raped by her father when she was only eleven years old. The father continued to rape Dana daily until he was sure she was pregnant. He and his wife (also a cultist) kept Dana hidden. When Dana's baby was born, the parents brought it to a secret cult meeting and sacrificed it on an altar. This gave them great prestige and power within the cult and inspired the father to impregnate Dana four more times before she was sixteen. Each time he murdered the babies as part of a satanic ritual.

Dana was so emotionally traumatized by the barbarian abuse she suffered, her mind no longer was willing to recognize and comprehend the ordeal. She totally suppressed all of her abuse. She left home in her late teens, found a job, and eventually was married and had two children. She remembered nothing of her life from age eleven through sixteen.

Then, when Dana's daughter was four and her son was two, Dana was reported to the police for child abuse. When the social workers came to find out why the daughter was covered with bruises, Dana confessed that one afternoon she had just gone berserk and had started beating her daughter.

Dana agreed to get psychological counseling. Her counselor eventually discerned that Dana had been abused and had blotted out an entire phase of her life. Dana was referred to Mary Battles, who served as Dana's therapist for the next three years.

"It was a slow and agonizing process to have Dana go back and face the hidden horror of those years," says Mary. "We had to take one memory at a time: a baby would be born, it would be killed. Dana would have to experience the rage and sorrow she had not been able to respond with when the abuse had originally happened. We relived the rape scenes, the pregnancies, the loss of the children. It was a horrendous ordeal, but a necessary one in order to help Dana not to unwillingly become a child abuser too."

Mary was pleased that Dana was able to recover after three years of therapy, and she feels that there is a lot of help available for SRA victims. There are many others, according to Mary, who are not as fortunate. She says many seem not to be able to release themselves from the control of the cult. They live in terror of being kidnapped or killed. Many SRA victims and counselors who have helped them have reported strange and frightening experiences along the pathway of trying to confront the truth.

"Cults are not comprised of teenagers on drugs and deranged lunatics," explains Mary Battles. "Their members include CEOs, lawyers, accountants, teachers, factory workers, even doctors and ministers. These people are tragically dysfunctional. Most abusers are people who were themselves abused as children. The cycle continues, and its circle of victims expands from one generation to the next. Research shows that phobic people attract phobic people. The problem feeds on itself."

RECOGNIZING SYMPTOMS

People suffering from ritual abuse are capable of displaying eight, ten, or twelve harmful symptoms. Among these symptoms, according to Mary, are promiscuity, uncontrollable anger, radical weight loss or weight gain, terrifying dreams, homosexuality, paranoia about being raped, undiagnosed pain, a sense of "feeling dirty", low self-esteem, inability to reach orgasm, memory loss, and a sense of social alienation. These people are unable to trust other people. If not treated properly, the outcome is disastrous.

Another of Mary Battles' patients, whom we'll call Rene, had started to show evidence of many of the above symptoms just after her husband died. Rene was sixty-two years old and had raised four children, all of whom were dysfunctional in one way or another. Rene, however, had always seemed quite normal . . . that is, while her husband was alive.

It turned out that Rene's husband had known that his wife had many serious problems—bouts of severe depression, rampages of anger, frequent nightmares—but he had sheltered her from society. He feared that if Rene was declared insane, he and Rene might have to give up their children to foster homes. He didn't want that, so he did what he could to help Rene maintain a low public profile.

What Rene's husband did not know was that Rene had been a victim of ritual abuse from age six to fourteen. She had buried those horrid experiences deep in her subconscious mind where she could not think consciously about them, but where they still were able to have a tremendous influence on all her decisions and behavior.

As a parent, when Rene would punish her children for doing something naughty, she would beat them savagely. She had no sense of proportion or perspective, for all she could "feel" instinctively was that children needed to be beaten. Her husband did his best to be with the children whenever they were home from school, for he knew the potential Rene had to hurt them. Rene, of course, had no way of knowing that as a child she had been beaten and tortured into total submission and that that experience had made her (the abused) into an abuser.

After Rene's husband died, there was no one to shield her behavior. The symptoms that had always been present but cautiously hidden were more exposed to everyone around Rene. Ironically, when people would ask Rene what was wrong with her, she would smile and say, "Nothing bad ever happens to me. Life is great!"

When Rene's behavior became too unmanageable, she sought treatment with Mary Battles.

"I had to use a variety of counseling techniques in order to get Rene to remember the abuse she had been submitted to as a child," explains Mary. "I asked her to start keeping a journal and to write about or draw pictures of whatever flashes of memory might come to her. I encouraged her to take time each day to relax, pray, and meditate about her life."

At first, Rene made very little progress, so Mary advanced to other counseling procedures.

"I told Rene to gather all the family photos she had of her parents, her siblings, her relatives, and herself," says Mary. "This became quite a project for her. She dug out scrapbooks, family albums, school yearbooks, newspaper clippings, and personal snapshots. I then assigned her to organize the photos in chronological order. Doing this revealed to Rene that there was a period of several years in her youth that she couldn't account for. This was a sobering dose of reality, but it certainly made her start taking her counseling sessions more seriously."

To revive long-suppressed memories, Mary had Rene sit down and force herself to remember her childhood home well enough to draw a basic blueprint of the floor plan. It took an hour, but Rene was able to do it. Next, Mary "walked" Rene through each room and asked Rene to describe the furnishings and decor. As Rene did this, shocking scenes suddenly appeared before her eyes. She saw adults surrounding her and using her in morbid ways as part of a cult ritual. These recollections were vibrantly traumatic, yet also emotionally redemptive. At last, the shame, pain, and fear that had so long festered in Rene's subconsciousness were now being confronted and released.

"Because Rene was sixty-two, most of the people she could recall as her abusers were either dead or people she'd lost contact with many years ago," says Mary Battles. "Despite these barriers, it was still vital that Rene have a chance to regain control of her life. So, I had her sit down and write a detailed letter to each one of those people who had abused her: her mother, her father, her aunt, her uncle, and two adult in-laws. Each letter exposed the abuser for what he or she was and gave details of how the ritual abuse had had vicious repercussions on Rene's later life. It also told the abuser that Rene would never again let someone take unfair advantage of her.

True, writing the letters was merely an exercise. Nevertheless, it gave Rene a sense of mastery over her life that she had never had before. It made her a new woman.

The saddest aspect of Rene's case is that her husband's

protective love for Rene and their girls was the very thing that prevented Rene from getting this sort of counseling much earlier.

BREAKTHROUGH TREATMENTS

Mary Battles and her colleagues at Alpha Counseling Centers have pioneered several procedures for helping people who are going through long periods of recovery from ritual abuse. Children are often too terrified to tell what happened to them. They've been threatened by their abusers and warned never to talk to "outsiders." As such, Mary will give a child a doll and will say, "Tell me some of the bad things that have been done to this doll lately." Often, the child will then relate his or her own stories of abuse.

Another procedure is to have peer counseling group meetings. Unlike traditional group therapy, however, the members of the ritual abuse recovery group may *only* talk about themselves. They cannot ask questions of others in the group or even make follow-up remarks. The whole function of the session is for the patient to realize three things: (1) other people are here who have gone through something similar to what I've gone through; (2) I can tell my story and share my burden without having to face any form of cross examination or criticism; and (3) I will be able to hear other people tell their stories and I will know that I am doing something good by sharing emotional support for someone in need.

If you ask Mary Battles if a 100 percent recovery is possible for the victims of ritual abuse, she will respond candidly, "There is recovery and there is improvement and there is hope. That doesn't mean that people will ever live with no residual effects of what they've experienced, but there can be steps in the right direction and there can be the day when some person's abuse will no longer dominate his or her life."

22

I Don't Remember Anything Before I Was Ten

The Possibility of Repressed Trauma

A lot of people need help for recovery from physical, emotional, or sexual abuse or neglect, but don't realize it because they don't remember it. Some people find this notion hard to believe, but it's widespread and it is important to recognize when it happens.

A child who is experiencing overwhelming pain and confusion can detach himself or herself from the awful reality of what is happening as a way of surviving. The child can virtually blank out the memory of what was so traumatic and painful. It's not done consciously or willingly. It happens as a defense to that which is so threatening and hard to comprehend. It's God's gift of survival to the traumatized child.

The problem is that it is only a way of temporarily coping and surviving, however, and not a way of living. It's like going into shock and, obviously, living in shock is not a pleasant way to live. Also, even though the memory of what happened may be repressed, that does not mean that the abuse or other trauma that is buried deep inside is not having an impact on that person's life. Quite the contrary. There are usually many, often intense consequences in the life of a person who is carrying repressed memories of emotional injury.

Janet is a woman who is admired and respected by those around her. She is attractive, educated, talented, and deeply committed to her family. Most people would never suspect that she would be included in the category of "victims." For most of her life, Janet would not have suspected that either. As a matter of fact, Janet had a close friend in her early adult years who had been molested by her father, and Janet always felt sorry for her friend and couldn't quite comprehend that something that awful could happen to anyone. If you had asked Janet whether anything under the heading of abuse had ever occurred in her life, she would have scoffed at the suggestion and convincingly said, "No!"

Deep inside Janet, however, were themes of pain that were, at times, almost too much to bear.

"Extending back into my childhood," Janet relates, "I recall that at bedtime I would pray that I would just live until the next morning. I was terrified of bedtime and of the darkness, and I lived in an almost continual expectation of dying in my sleep or of having someone break into my house and killing me. I never told anyone what I was feeling and never gave any outside evidence that I was feeling it. I didn't even realize that it was abnormal. I thought everyone went through some kind of fear, and it never occurred to me to talk about it."

Janet also came to realize that her childhood home was not the kind of place where you talked about feelings or any negative thoughts or experiences. That was one of the reasons she didn't talk about what was going on inside.

As Janet grew older, other problems developed. She became prone to depression. She was a driven perfectionist who discovered it was very difficult for her to be satisfied with very much around her. She had an eating disorder that she also didn't recognize. She alternated between being addicted to food and going on secret eating binges or going through periods when she stayed away from food and acted anorexic.

After she married, it also became apparent that sex was something in her life that was not going to work. On the one hand she hated sex and there were severe problems between her and her husband. On the other hand, she had impulses to have affairs and even toyed with experimenting with homosexuality. Even though she could not have a successful sexual relationship with her husband, she secretly masturbated much of the time and felt tremendous guilt about it.

"Things got so bad that I wanted to kill myself," Janet says. "By the time I was forty I had been to several counselors or physicians trying to relieve some of the symptoms I was experiencing, but it wasn't working and I just didn't want to live anymore."

The turning point for Janet came one evening while watching a television program. "It was a special about a woman whose father physically abused her when she was growing up. I started feeling queasy in my stomach during the show, and by the time it was over, it was all I could do to sit there and not let the other members of my family know that there was a volcanic explosion going on inside."

Janet took refuge in the bathroom, and while she was there the beginnings of long-repressed memories of being sexually abused by her father began to emerge. That prompted her to find a counselor who specialized in sexual abuse. Thus began a season of recovery that answered questions for Janet and her family that had long gone without answers. Janet's experience also affected her sister, who, it turned out, had been molested by her father as well but had not repressed the memories, although she had never told anyone about the experience and had never dealt with it.

The following list of statements covers some of the common experiences of those who have been the victim of abuse or some other kind of trauma from childhood and may have detached themselves from the memory of it. (Be sure to look at the self-tests from other chapters about abuse. If most of the questions from those chapters apply to the person you are concerned about but there are no memories of abuse, it bears some attention.) Put a check mark beside each statement that is true.

Assessing Repressed Trauma

☐ 1. This person has discovered that large gaps of memories are missing from childhood, such as from birth to kindergarten or from birth to junior high school or perhaps a period in between.

☐ 2. This person sometimes has intense and unexplained emotional or physical reactions to certain events or experiences or conversations or something that is seen or heard that might cause panic or revulsion.

☐ 3. This person lives in unexplained fear and dread of something awful happening, such as at night.

☐ 4. There was a time in this person's childhood when nightmares started occurring and continued repeatedly.

☐ 5. This person is either repulsed by sex or addicted to it, but he or she doesn't know why.

☐ 6. This person, even though having continuous memories all the way back to early childhood, has gaps in memories about certain people or places, such as not remembering anything about father or mother or school or a particular person's house.

☐ 7. This person knows that other members of the family, such as siblings, were abused, but says, "It didn't happen to me."

☐ 8. This person has suffered from depression that doesn't seem to have any reasonable explanation.

☐ 9. This person carries tremendous feelings of guilt.

☐ 10. There is a particular year in this person's growing up years when "everything changed" without apparent reason, such as suddenly being fearful of people or places or of the dark or suddenly becoming a behavior problem for the first time or suddenly starting to be a problem at school.

If you marked even one of the above statements, you need to consider seeking medical or psychological help. These are not meant to be absolute indicators of abuse or repressed trauma and are not a substitute for seeking counseling from a medical or psychological professional whom you trust.

UNDERSTANDING REPRESSED TRAUMA

There are a lot of questions in people's minds about repressed trauma. One is, "Do people who have memories of repressed abuse ever deceive themselves and make up memories?" In other words, "Can I trust repressed memories?"

In our experience the memories that emerge need to be taken seriously and are connected to something very painful and very scary that happened in that person's life.

It's important to realize that getting in touch with repressed memories is not simply a matter of saying, "Okay, I can imagine my uncle molesting me so therefore it must have happened." Actually, there are intense emotions and bodily sensations associated with memories of abuse that validate that they are real. There are also many different kinds of memories. There are visual memories, pictures of scenes from the past that are painful. There are also memories that are triggered by smells and odors. There are "body memories," where the body remembers and sometimes relives being pinned down or molested or beaten. When buried memories emerge, there will often be a combination of all those different kinds of memories. The experience for the victim, and for anyone who is with the victim, is very validating. A key to having assurance about recovered memories is when multiple kinds of memories confirm each other.

Even though the memories are real and are connected with genuine and painful experiences, there can sometimes be some confusion about the specifics. This is because these memories are often coming from the perspective of a very tiny and frightened person.

Anyone who has talked with a child who has just experienced a trauma knows that even though there is no doubt a trauma has taken place, it is going to be a challenge to get an adult picture of what happened. Very young children don't know how to describe someone as six feet tall or 180 pounds or as having wire-rimmed glasses. If, however, the abused child comes into the presence of the person who abused him or her, everyone will know it very quickly by the child's reaction. It's sometimes important to recognize that the emerging memories will be from the eyes and ears and body of a child at the age of the emotional injury.

Another common question is, "How quickly do the memories return and should I really concentrate on getting the memories?"

There is no way of predicting the timetable of recovery. It will be different and unique for each person. Our recommendation is: take it one step at a time and be content that you are making progress. You'll be able to catalog and document the timetable as you go along and then look back at it. It isn't realistic or effective to try to anticipate what will happen next and when it will happen.

Also, give yourself permission to discover whatever truth about yourself and your past and your family is there. Give yourself permission to recover any hidden memories and take whatever steps toward recovery you can, such as reading materials about recovery, finding a recovery group, or getting private counseling.

You don't need to be preoccupied with recapturing memories, however, or to be living in a state of constant frustration if they do not come on the schedule that you wish. There may be times when, in counseling, you have to deal with other issues as preparation for memories to emerge.

It's something like unpacking a duffel bag. If whatever you want is buried at the bottom, you need to go through all the other stuff to get there. Memories are often buried in layers, and you need to deal with whatever layer is at the top as a part of getting to each additional layer underneath.

Be courageous about dealing with what is there right now in terms of feelings and memories, and you'll be making progress.

PART FOUR:

Where Do I Go From Here?

What If I See Some of These Problems in My Own Life?

Many of you, as you have thumbed through this book, have seen yourself reflected on some of its pages. Some of you already knew that there might be a problem serious enough in your life to warrant taking steps to overcome it. Others of you may be facing the truth for the first time in regard to your problem areas.

We hope it has been of value to you to recognize that some of the most gripping and frustrating behaviors and conditions in our lives are actually symptoms of other things that we may need to deal with. In attempting to get well, it is very easy for us to become focused on the symptoms rather than the real problems underlying the symptoms.

Many people with various addictions have, for example, experimented with numerous ways of overcoming those addictions. They felt that if they could just cease the addictive behavior, then life would be worth living. The people around the addicts have felt the same way and have envisioned the day when the addict would stop his or her destructive behavior. This landscape of wishful thinking is strewn, however, with people who have tried and failed. And many of them have tried and failed over and over again.

It is a very significant day in the life of an addict or an

emotionally injured person when that person begins to realize that there is more to pay attention to than just the behavior or the condition that has seemed to cause so much
frustration. It is not only the addiction (or the fear or the guilt
or the anger) that needs to be dealt with, it is also the underlying injury that has typically resulted from physical, emotional, or sexual abuse or neglect or other kinds of emotional
injury.

This will be an important discovery on your part because it
will mean that the season of life you are now entering will be
a different one from before. It will mean that you will be trying to recognize that there has been emotional damage at the
deepest levels of your self. You will understand that the injury needs to be healed and that healing will occur only
through a season of recovery.

Perhaps you've described "recovery" in the past as simply
trying to overcome drinking or other addictive behaviors;
now, however, recovery is going to be defined at a deeper
level, and it will certainly include the goal of ending destructive behavior. More important, it will be focused on the healing that needs to occur for your damaged emotions.

THE STEPS TOWARD RECOVERY

There are several important steps you will need to take as
part of your personal recovery efforts:

First, *call it what it is.*

Ask God to help you be more honest about yourself and
about your life than you've ever been before. Try to identify
the behaviors, the conditions, or the experiences that are
true about your life and call them by their proper names.

If you are an alcoholic, then be courageous about admitting that to yourself and to others. If you have come to realize
that some of the experiences of your childhood are actually
under the umbrella of incest, then call them that. If you are
beginning to realize that the fear that has plagued your life is
actually evidence of having anxiety or panic attacks, then describe them that way to yourself and to others.

In other words, try to be as real as you can about your life and the lives of others around you. Make up your mind that, to the point of being as courageous as you can be, you are setting a goal to live each day in the real world.

This will be important for several reasons. For one thing, it will usher you in the direction of reality. For another thing, it will help you make specific choices for recovery.

Second, *realize that you can't do it alone.*

One of the most important things to grapple with at the beginning of your recovery is also one of the most difficult. This is the ability to recognize that you are probably not going to be able to overcome addictive behaviors or paralyzing conditions without the help and support of others. One of the common characteristics of a person who has experienced emotional injury is the tendency to want to be "alone" in his or her pain. There is a feeling that, "I can do this by myself" or "I will trust in the Lord and the Lord only, and I will not reach out to any other human beings for help."

That sounds like a step of faith, and for some people it is; but those are the words that can also come out of the mouth of someone who wants to avoid anything that might be threatening.

It has become a rule of recovery that you are not going to be able to achieve it by yourself. God has created us with the need for support and counsel and encouragement and understanding and correction. It is very important that our recovery include other people, especially people who will treat us with emotional safety and who will encourage us and understand us when we fail.

Third, *seek counseling or therapy.*

Some of your greatest help is going to come from a good counselor, especially someone who has a special understanding of your need. It is increasingly important to search for a counselor or a counseling center that seems to specialize in something that may be true about your life. It may be alcoholism or being the adult child of an alcoholic, or being a victim of molestation, or perhaps having an eating disorder. You need more than just a listening ear or a compassionate counselor. You need someone who has a special understanding of what you've gone through and what you're now still struggling with.

The best way to find a good counselor is to ask someone for a referral. If you know someone who has successfully gone through recovery and has had a good experience with a counselor, ask for a referral from that person. You can also get referrals from churches or from medical professionals. Additionally, you can look for support groups in your area that may have relationships with good counselors whom they can recommend. Should you need some referrals, call Alpha Counseling toll-free at 1–800–23Alpha. We keep lists of therapists and support groups.

OVERVIEW

In our next chapter we will discuss ways you can use the material in this book to be of help to other people. For now, however, the mirror is still reflecting *your* image. What do you see? How have this book's tests and lessons and insights enabled you to discover the problems and conditions that may be causing pain in your life?

You'll recall that at the beginning of this book we said you were going to walk down avenues of discovery. Some of those journeys may have been encouraging to you. Others may have been painful. The key thing to remember, however, is that recovery is possible. It just takes time and knowledgeable assistance. And the sooner you begin your season of recovery, the sooner you will start to heal.

If you are an addict, you've been living in a very tiny world emotionally. You need multiple sources of emotional nourishment: family, friends, school, jobs, plays, music, art, food, travel. Because of emotional injury or a dysfunctional home, however, we sometimes end up with only one or two sources for emotional nourishment. We end up living in an emotional closet, cut off from what could be rich and varied sources of emotional nourishment.

In that closet, we frantically try to find *anything* that seems nourishing and latch on to one or two things in order to satisfy all of our immense needs. For the addict, the addiction is sometimes the only reason for waking up in the morning.

When nothing else seems to be making sense or providing anything nourishing, sex or food or drugs or a hobby can be a reason for making it through the day. That's why it sometimes doesn't work to just go to an addict and say, "Stop that." The addict may go ahead and white knuckle it for a while, but when the addiction is taken away, what's left? For many addicts, nothing is left . . . and that's why the addiction will resume. An addict needs not only to control his or her behavior (a ceasing of the addiction), but also to allow multiple sources of emotional nourishment in his or her life.

Our book is here as a source of encouragement for you. You might occasionally go back and retake the tests you previously have taken. Watch for improvement. You'll see it, in time. Use the guidance and advice and suggestions in each chapter to help maintain your recovery efforts. Read other books too. We've provided reading lists in several chapters to assist you in finding help and encouragement in dealing with your specific problems. Spend time in prayer and Bible reading and draw strength from God's promises.

There are four important processes that you need to start following now: (1) Be as honest with yourself as you possibly can; (2) Be as honest with God as you possibly can; (3) Be as honest as you can with another person, a trusted person who has special understanding of what you've experienced; and (4) Enter into recovery, through counseling, recovery literature, and/or recovery groups.

Problems can be solved. Injured people can recover. Damaged relationships can be mended. Just by reading this book you have shown that you wanted to change your life in a positive way. Prior to this time, you didn't know how to go about it. You now have the guidance. Don't stop. We *know* you'll make it!

24

What If I See Some of These Problems in Another Person's Life?

We began with an overview of what you could expect to read in this book. We told you that you would be presented with an array of tests that would help you determine whether you or someone you are close to was having a problem serious enough to warrant attention.

You've now read and checked whatever tests you felt were appropriate to the conditions you are confronted with. If the tests have revealed that you, personally, need help, let us refer you to the preceding chapter. If, however, the tests have revealed that someone you are close to needs help, we'll discuss that now.

The cliché "You can lead a horse to water but you can't make it drink" applies to helping friends with problems. You may be eager to help, willing to provide support, anxious to encourage someone else to recover from a harmful condition; this, however, does not mean the other person is willing to cooperate.

It may anger or distress you to see another person continue to destroy his or her life when, with a little help, that person could be so different. Why, oh, *why* won't that individual take your advice and get help? The answer often lies in self-denial. Let us explain by using an illustration.

Rich Buhler has been a pilot and aircraft owner for many years and loves airplanes. He was once offered the opportunity to go through a physiological training program at a local U.S. Air Force base. It was a four-day seminar that taught Air Force personnel about some of the effects of flight on the body and how some of the choices we make about our bodies, such as whether to drink alcohol or smoke cigarettes or use drugs, can affect our ability to function safely in the air.

On the final day of the seminar, the students entered into an altitude simulation chamber where everyone was able to experience some of the things they had been studying in the classroom. One of the conditions that is important for a pilot to understand is hypoxia or "oxygen starvation." Various factors can contribute to a pilot experiencing oxygen starvation, all of which can, of course, hinder the pilot's ability to fly safely. Hypoxia can even result in a loss of consciousness.

The most intriguing thing about hypoxia is that when a person is first experiencing it, he doesn't realize it. This was graphically demonstrated in the altitude chamber.

Each of the students sat with a partner and each was given a clipboard with a piece of paper and a pencil. While the students kept the oxygen masks on, the altitude chamber simulated taking them to a height of 30,000 feet (where oxygen becomes very thin). When the students were given the signal, one partner took off his oxygen mask and started breathing the thinned air.

Under these conditions he would start to work on some simple math problems and essay questions that were on the sheets of paper everyone had been given. Rich was asked to sign his name. He was asked to do some simple arithmetic. He was asked very elementary questions, such as who was the first president of the United States. There was a sentence where he was supposed to go through and circle all of the capital letters and periods.

Each of the participants, of course, wanted to demonstrate his resilience by being able to do as many of the exercises on the sheet of paper as he could. Rich was happily responding to all of the instructions and was musing, "Hey, I'm really doing well because I am filling out more of the questions than my partner did."

Suddenly, Rich's partner reached for Rich's oxygen mask and began to force it onto his face. Rich was not happy about that because he felt that he was being cut off too quickly and that it was going to mess up his attempt to be the one who had gotten through more of the questions than anyone else in the altitude chamber.

Yes, Rich was genuinely annoyed when his partner grabbed his oxygen mask and put it on his face. But he took only two or three whiffs of normal oxygen before immediately realizing that his partner had done the right thing. In reality, Rich was probably on the verge of losing consciousness.

When he looked down at the piece of paper on his clipboard— which only a few seconds earlier had seemed so clear and crisp in his mind—he saw that on the final two or three questions his handwriting had become completely illegible. It was one of the most fascinating experiences of his life because he could remember just a moment before thinking that he had written the name "George Washington" flawlessly; now, however, he couldn't even read it.

This was a dramatic demonstration of the fact that there are conditions, like hypoxia, that a person can have without ever recognizing them. In fact, one of the symptoms that proves there is a problem is the person's adamant denial that he or she *does* have a problem! It's denial, pure and simple.

CONTINUOUS DENIAL EQUALS CONTINUOUS PROBLEMS

Anyone who has tried to help an addict or a person with one of the other conditions we have described in this book will understand exactly what Rich went through with the hypoxia. One of the characteristics of a person with an addiction or some other dysfunctional condition is that he or she doesn't seem to know it. Or if this person does know it, he or she is living in enough denial to discount the seriousness of the problem and to deny the need for help.

That, no doubt, is the experience of many people. There are people you know and love who are virtually living in another world. Your realm of reality is totally different from theirs. You probably have tried your best to convince this person of the seriousness of the problem in his or her life, but without success. It's one of the most frustrating experiences a good-intentioned person can have.

So what can you do? What steps can you take to help someone who has a problem but continually denies it?

It's good to begin by reminding yourself of the fact that this person may not be, as we have just described, living in the "real world." It's easy to become upset with a person in denial and to think of that person as being insensitive or unloving or uncaring, but this is seldom truly the case. Most people living in denial really do consider themselves to be loving spouses, committed parents, sincere Christians, and faithful friends. Most of them do not have any idea how much pain and sorrow they have caused the people around them. They are blind to it.

This is why it's important to realize that what you are primarily dealing with is a challenge of communication and not an attempt to shame someone. If you go to a husband, for instance, who is in denial and who views himself as being committed to his wife and you try to tell him that he has acted destructively or unfaithfully toward his wife, he will completely reject anything you have to say because that is *not* his view of himself.

It's important to begin by recognizing that what you're dealing with is a challenge of communicating to such people the nature and severity of what is going on. You won't succeed if you try to shame a person into recognizing her failure to be a true friend or a loving relative. Remember: she is blind to that.

SELF-EDUCATION

The opening recommendation we have is for you to become educated about the condition in the life of your friend or loved one. If you are dealing with an alcoholic, become an armchair expert on alcoholism. Do a lot of reading about it and discuss it with informed people. If you are living with someone with an eating disorder or someone who's a workaholic, do research on these addictions and the people who have these kinds of conditions.

These are plagues that have infected your home, your family, your friendships, or the place where you work. As such, it is going to make a lot of sense for you to become more aware of the kind of conditions that spawn such plagues and how they can be eradicated. Books, pamphlets, audio tapes, and videos are available from your local library, the Red Cross, the United Way, and area hospitals. They can inform you of causes of and treatments for various addictions and dysfunctions.

SUPPORT GROUPS

Increasing numbers of support groups are available for the friends and families of people whom we have described in this book. There are support groups for families of alcoholics and for those who have discovered themselves to be codependent with someone else's problems. There are support groups for families who have been ravished by drugs or gambling or sexual addictions.

It will be an enormous help for you to be able to get together with others who know exactly what you're going through and who have already discovered ways of responding to it. If misery loves company, trust us, recovery loves it even more.

COUNSELING

Even though the person you are codependent with is the one who seems more in need of counseling than you, it can be of enormous help if you take a step toward personal counseling. Find a counselor who is an expert on the kind of problem you are facing in your home or your friendship. That's the kind of person who will probably give you the greatest help with understanding about how to respond to this person. Besides, you deserve this sort of encouragement and support and compassion as compensation for the pain you are experiencing.

INTERVENTION SESSIONS

One of the choices that should be very seriously considered by family and friends of someone who is in denial is a process that is known as "intervention." An alcoholic, for example, is said to need to "reach bottom" before usually being willing to recognize the severity of the alcoholism. Intervention is a way of bringing the bottom up to where the alcoholic is, instead of waiting for him or her to reach bottom. Intervention also works well in dealing with other addictions and conditions in people's lives, such as post-traumatic stress disorder in military veterans.

The fascinating thing about intervention is that when it is properly done with a professional counselor, it is successful the vast majority of the times. Hardened alcoholics who have spent decades successfully resisting attempts on the part of those around them to get help will agree after intervention to enter, at last, into some kind of treatment program. An additional factor is that the typical intervention lasts only about ten or twenty minutes.

The power of the intervention is the result of several factors. One is that it is best done with the help of a professional counselor who is experienced at conducting interventions. Another is that those who participate in the intervention are people who are important to the addict, such as friends, family members, or co-workers. Another aspect is that those who will be participating in the intervention have been tutored in advance by the counselor; then, at the intervention, they are able to put into words some of the pain and loss that has occurred in their lives as a result of the addict's behavior.

An intervention is a loving confrontation. A successful intervention also includes a very clear communication to the addict of what is expected of him or her now, such as entering into treatment. The intervention also includes a very clear communication of what the consequences will be for the addict if he or she does not enter into treatment.

Probably the best way to find an intervention specialist is to call some of the counseling centers or hospitals in your area, particularly those that deal with alcoholics. They are the programs that make most use of this counseling procedure. The procedure may seem drastic, but the results are amazing.

CONCLUSION

You need to recognize that the problems you are facing in the life of a person who is near you are problems that this person is either not aware of or is in denial about. Blaming that person or accusing that person of not caring about those around him or her will probably not work. The addiction is not the problem, even though it produces a lot of problems of its own. The real problem is deeper and has to do with emotional pain. That's the level at which the person with the problem is going to have to deal with it.

The main challenge is one of communication, and communication, unfortunately, can sometimes only improve through crisis. You should educate yourself about the condition that's going on in this person's life, and you should not hesitate to find support groups or counselors who understand that kind of condition. Such groups can give you insight into the problem that will enable you to make some decisions about how to respond to it.

We have confidence in you. You *can* make a difference in other people's lives. Just keep this in mind: we are not here to see through people . . . we are here to see people through.

RECOMMENDED READING

ANGER

Blanchard, Charles A. *Getting Things from God: The Meaning of Christian Prayer.* Wheaton, IL: Victor Books, 1985.

Ferguson, Marilyn. *The Brain Revolution.* New York: Bantam Books, 1975.

LeTourneau, Richard. *Keeping Your Cool in a World of Tension.* Grand Rapids, MI: Zondervan Publishing House, 1971.

Lewis, David and James Greene. *Thinking Better.* New York: Rawson, Wade Publishers, 1982.

Lindsay, Peter H. and Donald A. Norman. *Human Information Processing.* New York: Academic Press, 1972.

Miller, Holly G. and Dennis E. Hensley. *How to Stop Living for the Applause.* Ann Arbor, MI: Servant Publishers, 1990.

DEPRESSION AND STRESS

Harper, Robert E. and Albert Ellis. *A New Guide to Rational Living.* North Hollywood, CA: Wilshire Publishing, 1975.

Hensley, Dennis E. *Staying Ahead of Time.* Indianapolis: R & R Newkirk Publishing, 1981.

Peck, M. Scott. *The Road Less Traveled.* New York: Touchstone, 1978.

Stoop, David. *Self-Talk: Key to Personal Growth.* Old Tappan, NJ: Revell, 1981.

Thurman, Chris. *The Truths We Must Believe.* Nashville: Thomas Nelson, 1991.

FOOD AND DRUGS

Beattie, Melody. *Codependent No More.* New York: Harper/Hazelden, 1987.

Johnson, Vernon. *I'll Quit Tomorrow.* New York: Harper & Row, 1973.

McCabe, Thomas. *Victims No More*. Center City, MN.: Hazelden Educational Materials, 1978.

Ohlemacher, Janet. *Desperate to be Needed—Freeing the Family from Chemical Codependency*. Grand Rapids, MI: Pyranee, 1990.

GAMBLING

Custer, Robert L. *When Luck Runs Out: Help for Compulsive Gamblers*. New York: Facts on File, 1985.

Estes, Ken. *Deadly Odds: The Compulsion to Gamble*. Newport, RI: Edgehill Publications, 1990.

Haskins, James. *Gambling—Who Really Wins?* New York: F. Watts Publishing, 1979.

Hyde, Margaret O. *Addiction: Gambling*. New York: McGraw Hill, 1978.

Olmstead, Charlotte. *Heads, I Win; Tails, You Lose*. New York: MacMillan, 1962.

GUILT

Douglass, Stephen B. *Managing Yourself*. San Bernardino, CA: Here's Life Publishers, 1978.

Frankl, Victor E. *Man's Search for Meaning*. New York: Pocket Books, 1980.

Haggai, John. *How to Win Over Worry*. Grand Rapids, MI: Zondervan, 1982.

Hensley, Dennis E. *How to Fulfill Your Potential*. Anderson, IN: Warner Press, 1989.

Kaiser, Walter C. *A Biblical Approach to Personal Suffering*. Chicago: Moody Press, 1982.

Scott, John R. W. *Your Mind Matters*. London: Inter-Varsity Press, 1972.

Waitley, Denis. *The Winner's Edge*. New York: Berkley Books, 1983.

WORKAHOLISM

Hensley, Dennis E. *Positive Workaholism: Making the Most of Your Potential*. Indianapolis: R & R Newkirk, 1983.

Minirth, Frank and Paul Meier. *The Workaholic and His Family: An Inside Look*. Grand Rapids, MI: Baker Books, 1981.

Narramore, Bruce and Bill Counts. *Freedom From Guilt*. Eugene, OR: Harvest House, 1976.

ADDITIONAL RESOURCES

Beattie, Melody. *Codependent No More*. New York: Harper/Hazelden, 1989.

Black, Claudia. *It Will Never Happen to Me*. New York: Ballantine, 1987. This is a book for adult children of alcoholics.

Buhler, Rich. *Pain and Pretending*. Nashville: Thomas Nelson Publishers, 1988.

Frank, Jan. *A Door of Hope: Recognizing and Resolving the Pains of the Past*. Ventura, CA: Here's Life Publishers, 1987. This book discusses incest and sexual abuse.

Forward, Susan and Craig Buck. *Betrayal of Innocence*. New York: Penguin Books, 1988. This book focuses on the topic of incest.

Fossum, Merle A. and Marilyn J. Mason. *Facing Shame*. New York: Norton Books 1989.

Hancock, Maxine and Karen Burton Mains. *Child Sexual Abuse: A Hope for Healing*. Chicago: Harold Shaw Publishers, 1987.

Larson, Gaylen. *Too Much Is Never Enough*. San Diego, CA: Pacific Press, 1992.

Minirth, Frank and Paul Meier. *Taking Control: New Hope for Substance Abusers and Their Families*. Grand Rapids, MI: Baker Book House, 1988.

Murray, Marilyn. *Prisoner of Another War*. Berkeley, CA: PageMill Press, 1991.

Payne, Leanne. *The Broken Image: Healing of the Homosexuality Crisis*. Wheaton, IL: Crossway Books, 1981.

Seamands, David. *Healing for Damaged Emotions*. Wheaton, IL: Victor Books, 1981.

Seamands, David. *Healing of Memories*. Wheaton, IL: Victor Books 1985.

SUPPORT GROUPS

WHERE TO FIND HELP FOR EATING DISORDERS

Anorexia Nervosa and Related Eating Disorders, P. O. Box 5102, Eugene, OR 97405, Phone: (503) 344-1144.

The American Anorexia/Bulimia Association, 418 East 76th Street, New York, NY 10021. Phone: (212) 734-1114.

The National Association of Anorexia Nervosa and Associated Disorders, Box 7, Highland Park, IL Phone: (708) 831-3438.

The Foundation for Education about Eating Disorders (FEED), P. O. Box 16375, Baltimore, MD 21210. Phone: (410) 467-0603.

The National Anorexic Aid Society, 1925 East Dublin Granville Road, Columbus, OH 43229. Phone: (614) 436-1112.

Overeaters Anonymous, P. O. Box 92870, Los Angeles, CA 90009. Phone: 1-800-743-8703.

ADDITIONAL SUPPORT AND RECOVERY GROUPS

Overcomers' Outreach, a network of 12-step groups dealing with various addictions and primarily associated with churches appealing to Christians. Write: 2290 West Whittier Boulevard, Suite A, La Habra, CA 90631. Phone: (310) 697-3994.

Real Active Survivor, providing help and networking for the survivor of ritual abuse. Write: P. O. Box 1894, Canyon Country, CA 91386. Phone: (805) 252-6437. Also provides information on multiple personality disorders.

Believe the Children, dealing with ritual abuse survivors. Write: P. O. Box 1358, Manhattan Beach, CA 90266.

VOICES (Victims of Incest Can Emerge Survivors) IN ACTION. Write: P. O. Box 148309, Chicago, IL 60614.

National Association of Children of Alcoholics, 31582 Coast Highway, Suite B, South Laguna, CA 92677.

National Association of Anorexia Nervosa and Associated Disorders, P. O. Box 7, Highland Park, IL 60601.

Overeaters Anonymous and Alcoholics Anonymous will be listed in your local telephone book.

Sex Addicts Anonymous, P. O. Box 3038, Minneapolis, MN 54403.

Phobia Society of America, P. O. Box 42514, Washington, DC 20015.

Self Help Clearing House, St. Clares-Riverside Medical Center, Pocono Road, Denville, New Jersey 07834. Ask for the *Self Help Sourcebook*, a guide to starting or finding help groups.

The National Council on Alcoholism and Drug Dependence. Phone: 1-800-475-HOPE.

Parents Anonymous, 6733 South Sepulveda Blvd. #270, Los Angeles, CA 90045. This is a national organization for parents who have abused or fear they might.